THE NEW
FLOWER
ARRANGER

THE NEW
FLOWER
ARRANGER

CONTEMPORARY APPROACHES TO
FLORAL DESIGN

TEXT BY
FIONA BARNETT
AND
ROGER EGERICKX

PHOTOGRAPHY BY
DEBBIE PATTERSON

HERMES
HOUSE

THIS EDITION IS PUBLISHED BY HERMES HOUSE, AN IMPRINT OF ANNESS PUBLISHING LTD, HERMES HOUSE, 88–89 BLACKFRIARS ROAD, LONDON SE1 8HA; TEL. 020 7401 2077; FAX 020 7633 9499

WWW.HERMESHOUSE.COM; WWW.ANNESSPUBLISHING.COM

IF YOU LIKE THE IMAGES IN THIS BOOK AND WOULD LIKE TO INVESTIGATE USING THEM FOR PUBLISHING, PROMOTIONS OR ADVERTISING, PLEASE VISIT OUR WEBSITE WWW.PRACTICALPICTURES.COM FOR MORE INFORMATION.

PUBLISHER: JOANNA LORENZ
TEXT: FIONA BARNETT AND ROGER EGERICKX
DESIGNER: NIGEL PARTRIDGE
PHOTOGRAPHER: DEBBIE PATTERSON

AUTHOR ACKNOWLEDGEMENTS
THE AUTHOR WOULD LIKE TO THANK ROGER EGERICKX AND RICHARD KISS OF DESIGN AND DISPLAY (SALES LTD) FOR THEIR GENEROUS PROVISION OF FACILITIES. WITH SPECIAL THANKS TO JENNY BENNETT FOR ALL HER HARD WORK.

ETHICAL TRADING POLICY

BECAUSE OF OUR ONGOING ECOLOGICAL INVESTMENT PROGRAMME, YOU, AS OUR CUSTOMER, CAN HAVE THE PLEASURE AND REASSURANCE OF KNOWING THAT A TREE IS BEING CULTIVATED ON YOUR BEHALF TO NATURALLY REPLACE THE MATERIALS USED TO MAKE THE BOOK YOU ARE HOLDING. FOR FURTHER INFORMATION ABOUT THIS SCHEME, GO TO WWW.ANNESSPUBLISHING.COM/TREES

PUBLISHER'S NOTE

CONTENTS

· · ·

INTRODUCTION

From an intricate corsage to a simple tied posy,
flower arranging requires care and consideration.
In the following pages advice is given on colour,
balance, scale and proportion, flower care, equipment, containers and using fruit and vegetables in
displays. Wiring techniques are also fully
explained, thereby enabling the reader to create
beautiful flower displays with confidence.

Right: These tulips create a wonderful domed effect which can be viewed from any side.

Below: A large Banksia cookinea *forms the focal point of this dried arrangement.*

Below: A wedding bouquet must be in scale with the person carrying it.

BALANCE

Balance is very important in a flower display, both physically and visually. Foremost, the flower arranger must ensure the physical stability of the display. This involves understanding the mechanics of the arrangement, the types and sizes of materials used, how they are positioned and in what type of container. Different types of floral displays require different strategies to ensure their stability.

A large arrangement to be mounted on a pedestal will need a heavy, stable container. The display materials should be distributed evenly around the container and the weight concentrated as near the bottom as possible. Make sure the longer flowers and foliage do not cause the display to become top-heavy.

A mantelpiece arrangement can be particularly difficult to stabilise since the display materials hanging down over the shelf will tend to pull it forward. So use a heavy container and position the flowers and foliage as far back in it as possible.

Check the stability of an arrangement at regular stages during its construction.

Achieving a visual balance in a flower arrangement involves scale, proportion and colour as well as creating a focal point in the display.

The focal point of an arrangement is an area to which the eye should be naturally drawn and from which all display materials should appear to flow. While the position of the focal point will vary according to the type of display, generally speaking it will be towards its centre. This is where the boldest colours and shapes should be concentrated, with paler colours around the outside.

Always think of the display in three dimensions, never forgetting that as well as a front, it will have sides and a back. This is not difficult to remember for a bouquet or a free-standing, pedestal-mounted display, but can be forgotten if a display is set against a wall. Even a flat-backed arrangement needs depth and shape. Recessing materials around the focal point will help give it depth and weight.

Balance in a floral display is the integration of all visual factors to create a harmonious appearance and with practice you will develop the ability to achieve this.

SCALE AND PROPORTION

Scale is a very important consideration when planning a floral display.

In order to create an arrangement which is pleasing to the eye, the sizes of different flower types used in the same display should not be radically different. For example, it would be difficult to make amaryllis look in scale with lily-of-the-valley.

The type of foliage used should be in scale with the flowers, the display itself must be in scale with its container, and the arrangement and its container must be in scale with its surroundings. A display in a large space in a public building must itself be appropriately large enough to make a statement, conversely a bedside table would require no more than an arrangement in a bud vase.

Proportion is the relationship of width, height and depth within a floral display and in this respect there are some rule-of-thumb guidelines worth bearing in mind.
❖ In a tied bouquet, the length of the stems below the binding point should be approximately one-third of the bouquet's overall height.

❖ In a trailing wedding bouquet, the focal point of the display will probably be about one-third of the overall length up from its lowest point.

❖ For a pedestal arrangement, the focal point will be approximately two-thirds of the overall height down from its topmost point.

❖ A vase with long-stemmed flowers such as lilies, should be around one-third the height of the flowers.

❖ The focal point of a corsage is about one-third the overall height up from the bottom.

However, remember that decisions on the scale and proportion of a floral display are a matter of personal taste and thus will vary from person to person.

The important thing is not simply to accept a series of rules on scale and proportion but to give these factors your consideration and develop your own critical faculties in this area.

Above: A contorted branch makes an unusual "trunk" for this dried topiary tree.

Top left: The heavy blossoms of white lilac are set against the darker stems of pussy willow and cherry.

COLOUR

The way in which colour is used can be vital to the success or failure of a display and there are several factors to bear in mind when deciding on a colour palette.

Though most people have an eye for colour, an understanding of the theory of colour is useful. Red, blue and yellow are the basic hues from which all other colours stem. Red, orange and yellow are warm colours which tend to create an exciting visual effect, while green, blue and violet are cooler and visually calmer.

Generally speaking, the lighter, brighter and hotter a colour, the more it will dominate an arrangement. White (which technically is the absence of colour) is also prominent in a display of flowers.

On the other hand, the darker and cooler the colour, the more it will visually recede into a display. It is important to bear this in mind when creating large displays to be viewed from a distance. In such circumstances blue and violet, in particular, can become lost in an arrangement.

Usually a satisfactory visual balance should be achieved if the stronger, bolder coloured flowers are positioned towards the centre of the display with the paler, more subtle colours around the outside.

Now armed with some basic knowledge of colour theory you can be braver in your choice of palette. "Safe" colour combinations such as creams with whites, or pinks with mauves have their place, but experiment with oranges and violets, yellows and blues, even pinks and yellows and you will add a vibrant dimension to your flower arranging.

Above: These bright yellow sunflowers are complemented by the brown contorted hazel twigs.

Left: The natural greens, yellows and mauves of these herbs blend perfectly together.

CONTAINERS

• • •

While an enormous range of suitable, practical, purpose-made containers is available to the flower arranger, with a little imagination alternatives will present themselves, often in the form of objects we might not have at first glance expected. An old jug or teapot, a pretty mug that has lost its handle, an unusual-looking tin, a bucket, a jam jar, all these offer the arranger interesting opportunities.

Remember, if the container is for fresh flowers, it must be watertight or properly lined. Consider the scale and proportion of the container both to the particular flowers you are going to use, and the type of arrangement.

Do not forget the container can be a hidden part of the design, simply there to hold the arrangement, or it can be an integral and important feature in the overall arrangement.

BAKING TINS (PANS)
Apart from the usual round, square or rectangular baking tins (pans), a number of novelty shapes are available. Star, heart, club, spade and diamond shaped baking tins (pans) are used to make cakes that are out of the ordinary and they can also be used very effectively to produce interesting flower arrangements.

These tins (pans) are particularly good for massed designs, either of fresh or dried flowers, but remember, the tin may need lining if it is being used for fresh flowers.

BASKETS
Baskets made from natural materials are an obvious choice for country-style, informal displays. However, there is a wide range of basket designs available to suit many different styles.

Large baskets are good for table or static displays while smaller baskets

Massed dried flowerheads in this baking tin (pan) produce a striking display.

with handles can be carried by bridesmaids or filled with flowers or plants and made into lovely gifts. Traditional wicker baskets can be obtained which incorporate herbs or lavender in their weave.

Wire or metal baskets offer an ornate alternative to wicker and twig, since the wire can be formed into intricate shapes and also can have a more modern look.

CAST-IRON URNS
More expensive than many other types of container, the investment in a cast-iron urn is repaid by the splendid classic setting it offers for the display of flowers. Whether the arrangement is large and flowing or contemporary and linear, the visual strength of a classical urn shape will provide the necessary underpinning.

Of course the physical weight of a cast-iron urn is a factor to consider; it is a plus in that it will remain stable with the largest of displays but a minus when it comes to moving it!

ENAMELLED CONTAINERS
The appeal of using an enamelled container probably lies in the bright colours available. Containers in strong primary colours work well with similarly brightly coloured flowers to produce vibrant displays.

GALVANIZED METAL BUCKET AND POT
The obvious practical advantage of galvanized metal containers is that they will not rust. The attractive silvered and polished texture is ideal for contemporary displays in both fresh and dried flowers.

Today lots of shapes and sizes of containers are available with a galvanized finish but even an old-fashioned bucket can be used to good effect in flower arranging.

GLASS VASES
A glass vase is often the first thing that springs to mind for flower arranging. And indeed, there is an enormous range of purpose-made vases available.

The proportions of this design give prominence to the classical urn.

A varied selection from the vast range of containers that can by used for flower arranging

Particularly interesting to the serious flower arranger will be simple clear glass vases which are made in all the sizes and geometric shapes you could ever need. Their value lies in their lack of embellishment which allows the arrangement to speak for itself. Remember the clear glass requires that the water be changed regularly and kept scrupulously clean, since below the water is also part of the display.

There are also many other forms of vase – frosted, coloured, textured, and cut glass – and all have their place in the flower arranger's armoury.

PITCHERS

Pitchers of all types are ideal flower receptacles. Ceramic, glass, enamelled or galvanized metal; short, tall, thin, fat – whatever their shape, size or colour, they offer the flower arranger a wide range of options.

Displays can range from the rustic and informal to the grand and extravagant, depending on your choice of pitcher and materials.

PRE-FORMED PLASTIC FOAM SHAPES

Clean to handle, convenient to use, pre-formed plastic foam comes in a wide range of shapes and sizes such as circles, crosses, rectangles and even "novelty" designs like stars, numerals, hearts and teddy bears. Each shape is a moisture-retaining foam with a watertight backing. Equivalent foam shapes are available for dried flowers.

Although often associated with funeral and sympathy designs, pre-formed plastic foam shapes also offer the flower arranger a variety of bases for many other types of display.

TERRACOTTA PLANT POTS

Traditional or modern, the terracotta pot can be utilized to hold an arrangement of flowers and not just plants. If the arrangement is built in plastic foam, line the pot with cellophane (plastic wrap) before

inserting the foam, to prevent leakage. Alternatively just pop a jam jar or bowl into the pot to hold the water.

The appearance of terracotta pots can be changed very effectively by techniques such as rubbing them with different coloured chalks, or treating them with gold leaf. They can also be aged by the application of organic materials such as sour milk which, if left, will enable a surface growth to develop.

WOODEN TRUGS AND BOXES

Old-fashioned wooden trugs and seedboxes can make charming and effective containers for floral displays. Their rustic appeal makes them particularly suitable for informal country-style designs where the container is an enhancing feature. Rubbing the surface of a wooden container with coloured chalk can create an entirely new look.

Of course you must remember to line the box with waterproof material if fresh flowers or plants are going to be used in the display.

EQUIPMENT

· · ·

The flower arranger can get by with the minimum of equipment when he or she is just starting out. However, as he or she becomes more adventurous, a selection of specialized tools and equipment will be useful. This section itemizes those pieces of equipment used in the projects contained in the book.

CELLOPHANE (PLASTIC WRAP)

As wrapping for a bouquet, cellophane (plastic wrap) can transform a bunch of flowers into a lovely gift, and it has a more practical use as a waterproof lining for containers. Also, it can look very effective scrunched up in a vase of water to support flower stems.

FLORIST'S ADHESIVE

This very sticky glue is supplied in a pot and is the forerunner to the hot, melted adhesive of the glue gun. It is necessary when attaching synthetic ribbons or other materials which might be adversely affected by the heat of a glue gun.

FLORIST'S ADHESIVE TAPE

This is a strong adhesive tape used to secure plastic foam in containers. Although it will stick under most circumstances, avoid getting it too wet as this will limit its adhesive capability.

PLASTIC FOAM

Plastic foam comes in a vast range of shapes, sizes and densities, and is available for both dry and fresh flowers. While the rectangular brick is the most familiar, other shapes are available for specific purposes.

Plastic foam is lightweight, convenient to handle and very easy to cut and shape with just a knife. A brick of plastic foam for fresh flowers soaks up water very quickly

Before starting to build a design make sure you have all the materials close to hand.

(approximately 1½ minutes) but must not be resoaked as the structure alters and its effectiveness will be reduced. Plastic foam for dried flowers can seem too hard for the delicate stems of some flowers but a softer version is available, so consider which type you need before starting the design.

FLORIST'S SCISSORS

A strong, sharp pair of scissors are the flower arranger's most important tool. As well as cutting all those things you would expect, the scissors must also be sturdy enough to cut woody stems and even wires.

FLORIST'S TAPE
(STEM-WRAP TAPE)

This tape is not adhesive, but the heat of your hands will help secure it to itself as it is wrapped around a stem

The tape is used to conceal wires and seal stem ends. It is made either from plastic or crêpe paper and it will stretch to provide a thin covering. The tape is available in a range of colours although green is normally used on fresh flowers.

FLORIST'S WIRE

Wire is used to support, control and secure materials, also to extend stems and to replace them where weight reduction is required. The wire tends

to be sold in different lengths. Most of the projects in this book use 36 cm (14 in) lengths. Always use the lightest gauge of wire you can while still providing sufficient support. The most popular gauges are:

1.25mm (18g)	0.28mm (31g)
0.90mm (20g)	0.24mm (32g)
0.71mm (22g)	Silver reel
0.56mm (24g)	*(rose) wires:*
0.46mm (26g)	0.56mm (24g)
0.38mm (28g)	0.32mm (30g)
0.32mm (30g)	0.28mm (32g)

Make sure that the wires are kept in a dry place because any moisture will cause them to rust.

GLOVES

While some flower arranging processes would be impeded by gloves, it makes sense to protect your hands whenever necessary, especially if handling materials with sharp thorns or sap which might irritate the skin. So keep some domestic rubber gloves and heavy-duty gardening gloves in your florist's workbox.

GLUE GUN

The glue gun is an electrically powered device fed by sticks of glue, which it melts to enable the user to apply glue via a trigger action. In floristry it is a relatively recent development but invaluable in allowing the arranger to attach dried or fresh materials to swags, garlands or circlets securely, cleanly and efficiently.

The glue and the tip of the gun are extremely hot, so take care at all times when using a glue gun. Never leave a hot glue gun unattended.

PAPER RIBBON

Paper ribbon is an alternative to satin and synthetic ribbon and is available in a large range of mostly muted, soft

colours. It is sold twisted and rolled up. Cut the length of ribbon required in its twisted state and carefully untwist and flatten it to its full width before creating your bow.

PINHOLDER

The pinholder is a heavy metal disc approximately 2 cm (¾ in) thick which has an even covering of sharp metal pins, approximately 3 cm (1¼ in) long. Pinholders are available in a range of diameter sizes for different displays.

The pinholder is placed under the water and the bottom of the flower stems are pushed on to the pins. The weight of the stems is balanced by the weight of the pinholder. It is ideal for creating *Ikebana*-style displays or twiggy linear arrangements.

RAFFIA

A natural alternative to string and ribbon, raffia has several uses for the flower arranger. It can be used, a few strands at a time, to tie together a hand-arranged, spiralled bunch, or to attach bunches of dried or fresh

Start with the basic equipment and add items as your skill develops.

flowers to garlands and swags. In thicker swathes it can also be used to finish bouquets and arrangements by tying them off and being formed into decorative bows.

ROSE STRIPPER

This ingenious little device is a must when handling very thorny roses. Squeeze the metal claws together and pull the stripper along the stem, and the thorns and leaves will be removed. There is also a blade attachment to cut stem ends at an angle. Always wear thick gardening gloves.

SATIN RIBBON

Available in a large variety of widths and colours, satin ribbon is invaluable to the flower arranger when a celebratory final touch is required.

Satin ribbon is preferable to synthetic ribbon because it looks and feels so much softer. Its only drawback is that it frays when cut.

SECATEURS (GARDEN CLIPPERS)

These are necessary to cut the tougher, thicker stems and branches of foliage. Always handle scissors and secateurs with care and do not leave within the reach of young children.

TWINE

String or twine is essential when tying spiralled bunches, making garlands or attaching foliage to gates and posts.

WIRE MESH

Although plastic foam now offers much more flexibility for the flower arranger, wire mesh still has its place in the florist's armoury.

When creating large displays, wire mesh is essential to strengthen the plastic foam and prevent it from crumbling when large numbers of stems are pushed into it. The mesh should be cut in lengths from the roll, crumpled slightly, laid over the top and wrapped around the sides of the foam and wedged between it and the container, then secured in place with florist's adhesive tape.

TECHNIQUES
· · ·

TAPING

Stems and wires are covered with florist's tape (stem-wrap tape) for three reasons: first, cut materials which have been wired can no longer take up water and covering with tape seals in the moisture that already exists in the plant; second, the tape conceals the wires, which are essentially utilitarian, and gives a more natural appearance to the false stem; third, wired dried materials are covered with florist's tape (stem-wrap tape) to ensure that the material does not slip out of the wired mount.

1 Hold the wired stem near its top with the end of a length of florist's tape (stem-wrap tape) between the thumb and index finger of your left hand (or the opposite way if you are left-handed). With your other hand, hold the remainder of the length of tape at 45° to the wired stem, keeping it taut. Starting at the top of the stem, just above the wires, rotate the flower slowly to wrap the tape around both the stem and wires, working down. By keeping it taut, the tape will stretch into a thin layer around the stem and wires. Each layer should overlap and stick to the one before. You may add flowerheads at different heights as you tape to create units. Finally, fasten off just above the end of the wires by squeezing the tape against itself to stick it securely.

MAKING A STAY WIRE

1 Group together four .71 wires, each overlapping the next by about 3 cm (1¼ in). Start taping the wires together from one end using florist's tape (stem-wrap tape). As the tape reaches the end of the first wire add another .71 wire to the remaining three ends of wire and continue taping, and so on, adding wires and taping four together until you achieve the required length of stay wire.

SINGLE LEG MOUNT

This is for wiring flowers which have a strong natural stem or where a double weight of wire is not necessary to support the material.

1 Hold the flowers or foliage between the thumb and index finger of your left hand (opposite way if you are left-handed) while taking the weight of the material across the top of your hand. Position a wire of the appropriate weight and length

behind the stem about one-third up from the bottom. Bend the wire ends together with one leg shorter than the other. Holding the short wire leg parallel with the stem, wrap the long wire leg firmly around both the stem and the other wire leg several times. Straighten the long wire leg to extend the stem. Cover the stem and wire with florist's tape (stem-wrap tape).

DOUBLE LEG MOUNT

This is formed in the same way as the single leg mount but extends the stem with two equal length wire legs.

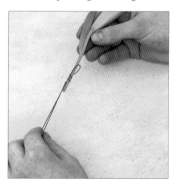

1 Hold the flower or foliage between the thumb and index finger of your left hand (or opposite way if you are left-handed) while taking the weight of the plant material across the top of your hand. Position a wire of appropriate weight and length behind the stem about one-third of the way up from the bottom. One-third of the wire should be to one side of the stem with two-thirds to the other. Bend the wire parallel to the stem. One leg will be about twice as long as the other.

Holding the shorter leg against the stem, wrap the longer leg around both stem and the other wire to secure. Straighten both legs which should now be of equal length.

PIPPING

Pipping is the process whereby small flowerheads are removed from a main stem to be wired individually. This process can be used for intricate work with small delicate plant materials.

1 Bend a thin silver wire into a hairpin about its centre and twist at the bend to form a small loop above the two projecting legs.

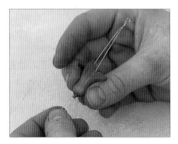

2 Push the legs into the flower centre, down through its throat, and out of its base to create a stem.

3 Using more silver wire, double leg mount this stem with any natural existing stem, and tape if required.

UNITS

A unit is the composite stem formed from two or more pieces of plant material. Units of small flowers can be used in corsages and hair-comb decorations, and units of larger flowers in wired wedding bouquets.

Units should be made up of one type of material only. For small units, first wire and tape the individual flowerheads, buds or leaves.

Start with the smallest of the plant material and attach a slightly larger head to it by taping the wires together. Position the larger head in line with the bottom of the first item. Increase the size of the items as you work downward.

For units of larger flowers you may have to join the wire stems by double leg mounting them with an appropriate weight of wire before taping.

EXTENDING THE LENGTH OF A STEM

Flowerheads with short stems, and flowers that are delicate may need the extra support of an extended stem. There are two methods of extending a stem.

Wire the flowerhead using the appropriate method and correct

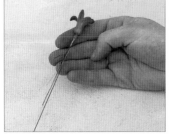

weight of wire. Then single leg mount the wired flowerhead using a .71 wire and tape the wires and any natural stem with florist's tape (stem-wrap tape).

Alternatively, push a .71 wire into the base of the flowerhead from the bottom, then at right angles to this push through a .38 silver wire from one side to the other.

Bend the .38 silver wire so that the two ends point downwards, parallel to the .71 wire. Wrap one leg of .38 wire firmly around its other leg and the .71 wire. Cover with florist's tape (stem-wrap tape).

WIRING AN OPEN FLOWERHEAD

This is a technique for the wiring of individual heads of lily, amaryllis and tulip and is also suitable for small, soft or hollow-stemmed flowers such as anemones and ranunculus.

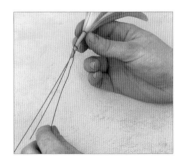

Cut the stem of the flower to around 4 cm (1½in). Push one .71 wire up through the inside of the stem and into the base of the flowerhead. Double leg mount the stem and its internal wire with a .71 wire. Tape the stem and wire.

The internal wire will add strength to the flower's natural stem and the double leg mount will ensure that the weight of the flowerhead is given sufficient support.

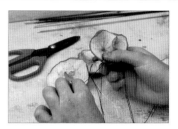

Preserved (dried) apple slices require careful handling when wiring.

WIRING A ROSE HEAD

Roses have relatively thick, woody stems so to make them suitable for use in intricate work, such as buttonholes, headdresses and corsages, the natural stem will need to be replaced with a wire stem.

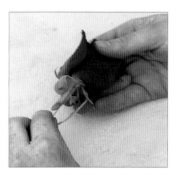

Cut the stem of the rose to a length of approximately 3 cm (1¼ in).

Push one end of a .71 wire through the seed box of the rose at the side. Holding the head of the rose carefully in your left hand (opposite way if left-handed), wrap the wire several times firmly around and down the stem. Straighten the remaining wire to extend the natural stem. Cover the wire and stem with florist's tape (stem-wrap tape).

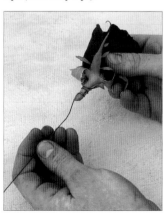

WIRING FRUIT AND VEGETABLES

Using fruit and vegetables in swags, wreaths and garlands, or securing them in plastic foam displays will require wiring them first. The method will depend on the item to be wired and how it is to be used.

Heavy fruits and vegetables, such as oranges, lemons or bulbs of garlic, will need a heavy .71 wire or even .90. The wire should be pushed through the item, just above its base from one side to the other. Push another wire through the item at right angles to the first and bend all four projecting wires to point downwards.

Depending on how the fruit or vegetables will be used, either cut the wires to a suitable length to be pushed into plastic foam, or twist the wires together to form a single stem.

Small delicate fruits and vegetables such as mushrooms or figs need careful handling as their flesh is easily damaged. They normally only need one wire. Push the wire through the

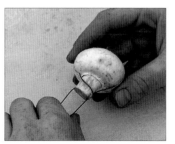

base of the item from one side to the other and bend the two projecting wires downwards. Depending on how the material is to be used, either twist to form a single stem, or trim to push into plastic foam.

For the soft materials .71 is the heaviest weight of wire you will require. In some instances, fruit or vegetables can be attached or secured in an arrangement by pushing a long wire "hairpin" right through the item and into the plastic foam behind.

Fruit or vegetables that have a stem, such as bunches of grapes or artichokes, can be double leg mounted on their stems with appropriate weight wires.

Extend the length of a starfish by double leg mounting one of its legs.

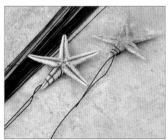

FRUIT AND VEGETABLES IN FLOWER DISPLAYS

The colours and textures of fruit and vegetables can provide harmony or contrast to enhance flower arrangements. The acid colours of citrus fruits, and autumn tints of apples and pears are all readily available to the flower arranger.

Some fruits such as pomegranates, passion fruits and blood oranges are particularly attractive when they have

The strong forms of fruit and vegetables lend themselves well to displays such as this wall swag (above) and unusual obelisk (right). Careful wiring ensures the materials stay in position.

been cut or torn open to reveal their flesh. However, remember that open fruits will deteriorate quickly so only use them for short-term displays at special events, parties or dinners.

Vegetables might seem a surprising choice for use in flower arrangements but the subtle colours and textures can be combined with blooms to beautiful effect. Purple artichokes, almost black aubergines (eggplants), pink and white garlic bulbs, and bright red radishes can give depth, substance and a focal point to a variety of differnt arrangements.

Dried citrus fruit slices look wonderful, and will retain a slight tangy perfume.

COVERING A WIRE HANDLE WITH RIBBON

To make carrying a wired bouquet more comfortable the wired stems can be made into a handle.

1 To ensure that the handle is the correct length, trim it to about 1.5 cm (½in) longer than the diagonal measurement across your palm. Cover the wire handle with florist's stem-wrap tape. Hold the bouquet in your left hand (opposite way if left-handed) and, with your thumb, trap a long length of 2.5 cm (1 in) wide ribbon against the binding point of the bouquet, leaving 10 cm (4 in) of ribbon above your thumb.

Take the long end of the ribbon down the handle, under its end and approximately half way up the other side. Hold it in place there with the little finger of your left hand, making sure that your thumb remains firmly in place at the binding point.

2 Wind the ribbon back over itself, around and down the handle to its end. Next wind the ribbon back up the handle all the way to the binding point, covering the ribbon already in place and the tape on the handle.

3 Take the winding end of the ribbon, and the excess 10 cm (4 in) at the other end, and tie in a knot at the binding point. Finish in a bow and trim the ribbon ends.

LINING A CONTAINER

If a container is to be used for arranging fresh flowers then clearly it must be watertight. However, if you are arranging your flowers in plastic foam then you can use a container which is not watertight provided you line it with polythene or cellophane (plastic wrap).

Cut a piece of cellophane (plastic wrap) slightly larger than the container and push it into the container making sure that it gets into all the corners and has no holes or tears. Cut the soaked plastic foam with a knife to fit the container and wedge it in. Trim the lining around the edge of the container and secure the plastic foam in place with florist's adhesive tape.

Be sure not to allow any water to get between the lining and the container and do not trim the lining too short as the water may spill over the top and down on to the sides.

SPIRALLING STEMS

A hand-tied spiralled bouquet is an excellent way of presenting flowers as a gift because they are already arranged and the recipient only has to cut the string and place the flowers in a suitable vase.

1 Place all the materials close to hand so that you can pick up individual stems easily. Hold a strong stem of foliage or flowers in your left hand (opposite if left-handed) approximately two-thirds down from its top. Build the bouquet by adding one stem of your materials at a time, turning the bunch in your hand as you do so to produce a spiral of stems. If you add your materials in a pre-planned repeating sequence, it will ensure an even distribution of different varieties throughout the bouquet. By occasionally varying the position you hold the stems as you add them you can create a domed shape to the bunch.

2 When you have completed the bunch tie securely with twine, raffia or ribbon around the point where all the stems cross – the binding point.

3 Trim the stem ends so they are even, remembering that the stems below the binding point should comprise about one-third of the overall height of the finished bouquet.

STITCHING LEAVES

Stitching is a technique for wiring a leaf in such a way that it can be held in a "naturally" bent position.

Hold a leaf in your left hand with its back facing you (opposite way if you are left-handed) and stitch a thin wire horizontally through the central vein and back out again.

Bend the legs of the wire down along the stem forming a hairpin shape. Hold one leg of wire against the stem of the leaf and wrap the other leg of wire around both stem and wire several times. Then straighten the legs and tape if required.

Below: Very fine reel wire can also be used to secure flowers and foliage to wreaths and basket edgings.

New Ways with Fresh Flowers

· · ·

From an abundant armful of glorious old-fashioned roses in full bloom in a jug, to the subtle simplicity of woodland berries in a tinted glass, every flower arrangement you compose is an expression of your personality and artistic style. The following pages will help you to make the very most of fresh flowers, in both classic and informal compositions.

INTRODUCTION
· · ·

*Above: Lily and Hyacinth
Planted Basket (page 70)*

*Below: Summer Basket
Display (page 65)*

The vagaries of fashion have had their impact on flower arranging just as they have on most other aspects of life. However, one discernible long-term trend has been a relaxation of the formal approach of 20 years or more ago when flowers sometimes looked as though they had been beaten into submission!

Nowadays, the straightjacket of formality has been replaced by an emphasis on the flowers themselves creating the impact in a natural way.

No longer restricted by a set of rigid rules, the flower arranger is free to take inspiration from anything that triggers the creative process, it may be the decor of a room or a particular type of container, but equally it could just be the mood of the moment or even the state of the weather!

Of course, modern flower arranging still relies on the basic principles of colour, scale, proportion and balance but it uses these to create more adventurous designs in exciting colour combinations and textures. It is also concerned with simplicity, and today the flower arranger is as likely to create a successful display with daffodils in a jam jar as with an opulent arrangement on a pedestal.

Flower arranging has become the art of understanding the materials and getting the best out of them with the minimum complication.

One of the single most important factors in allowing the flower arranger more

Above: Fruit and Flower
Swag (page 44)

Left: Arum Lily Vase
(page 87)

Below: Tulip Topiary Tree
(page 68)

creative freedom has been the enormous improvement in the availability and good quality of commercially grown cut flowers.

The flower arranger is no longer restricted by the seasonal availability of the majority of popular cut blooms and has an ever-growing range of flowers to work with. Further, modern growing techniques have improved the quality and increased the life span of cut flowers, for example the few days' cut life of sweet peas has been extended to a week or more.

All of these improvements give today's flower arranger more options in terms of choice of materials, colour palette and arranging techniques.

To some, flower arranging is an all-consuming passion but to many it remains a mystery. In reality, it is an activity in which most people can, to a greater or lesser extent, successfully participate. All you need is a working knowledge of the contents of this book coupled with a little determination, some imagination and lots of practice. The important thing to remember is that flower arranging is a creative, not just a physical, process.

CARE OF CUT FLOWERS

· · ·

approximately 6 cm (2½ in) and plunge the bottoms of the stems into the hot water, leaving them for two to three minutes before removing and plunging them into deep cold water. The heat of the boiling water will have dispelled air from the stems to enable the efficient take-up of cold water. The boiling water will also have destroyed bacteria on the stem ends.

Wilted roses can also be revived by having their stems recut and given the boiling water treatment, and then left standing (with their heads wrapped up to their necks) in cold water for two hours.

The rose stripper (below) is invaluable when dealing with very thorny stems.

Conditioning

Conditioning is the term for the process of preparing flowers and foliage for use in arranging.

The general rules are: remove all lower leaves to ensure there is no soft material below the water level where it will rot, form bacteria and shorten the life of the arrangement; cut the stem ends at an angle to provide as large a surface area as possible for the take-up of water; and, finally, stand all materials in cold water for a couple of hours to encourage the maximum intake of water before use.

For many varieties of flower and foliage this treatment is perfectly adequate; for some, however, there are a number of additional methods to increase their longevity.

Boiling Water

The woody stems of lilac, guelder rose and rhododendron, the sap-filled stems of milkweed (euphorbia) and poppy, even roses and chrysanthemums, will benefit from the shock treatment of immersing their stem ends in boiling water.

Remove all lower foliage, together with approximately 6 cm (2½ in) of bark from the ends of woody stems. Cut the stem ends at an angle of 45 degrees and, in the case of woody stems, split up to approximately 6 cm (2½ in) from the bottom. Wrap any flowerheads in paper to protect them from the hot steam.

Carefully pour boiling water into a heatproof container to a depth of

Searing

Searing is a method of extending the lives of plants such as milkweed (euphorbia) and poppies which contain a milky sap, the release of which affects the water quality.

It involves passing the stem end through a flame until it is blackened, then placing it in tepid water. This forms a layer of charcoal to seal the stem end, preventing sap leakage but still allowing the take-up of water.

HOLLOW STEMS

Delphiniums, amaryllis and lupins have hollow stems and the best method of conditioning them is to turn them upside-down and literally fill them with water.

To keep the water in the stem, form a plug from cotton wool or tissue and carefully bung the open stem end. Tie a rubber band around the base of the stem to avoid splitting, then stand the stem in tepid water. The water trapped inside the stem will keep it firm and the cotton wool will help draw more water up into it.

FOLIAGE

Generally the rules for conditioning foliage are the same as for flowers. It is vital to strip the lower leaves and cut the stem base at an angle. Depending on the stem structure and size, other special techniques may well apply. It is also important to scrape the bark from the bottom 6 cm (2½ in) of the stem

and split it to further encourage the take-up of water and thereby prolong the life of the foliage.

WRAPPING TO STRAIGHTEN STEMS

Some flowers, such as gerbera, have soft, flexible weak stems and other flowers may simply have wilted. There is a technique for strengthening such material: take a group of flowers and wrap the top three-quarters of

their stems together in paper to keep them erect, then stand them in deep cool water for about two hours. The cells within the stems will fill with water and be able to stand on their own when the paper is removed.

ETHYLENE GAS

Ethylene is an odourless gas emitted by such things as rubbish (garbage), exhaust fumes, fungi and ripening fruit. It has the effect of accelerating the rate at which some flowers mature which in turn causes non-opening and dropping of buds and yellowing of leaves. Particularly susceptible are carnations, freesia, alstroemeria and roses. Be aware of this when using fruit in a flower arrangement.

FLOWER AVAILABILITY CHART
• • •

This list is an indication of current availability of the flowers from the Dutch market.
As development in production of individual varieties improve, this information may change.
*** *good availability* ** *some availability* * *limited availability*

Flower Type	Jan	Feb	Mar	Apr	May	Jun	Jul	Aug	Sep	Oct	Nov	Dec	Special Notes
Achillea			*	*	*			***	***				Some varieties only available in Spring
Aconitum (monkshood)					*			***	***				
Agapanthus	*	*						***	***	*	*	*	Some varieties moderately available in Winter
Ageratum		*			*			***	***	***	***		
Alchemilla (mollis)							*	*					
Allium					*			***	***				
Alstroemeria	***	**	**	***	***	***	***	***	***	***	***	***	Some varieties not so available early Spring
Amaranthus (red and green)	**					**	**	***	***	***	***	***	
Amaryllis (Belladonna)	**							**	**	***	***	***	
Ammi majus (white dill)	***	***	***	***	***	***	***	**	**	***	***	***	
Anemones	***	***	***	***	***	***	***			***	***	***	
Anethum graveolens (green dill)	**				**			**	**	***	***		
Anigozanthus (kangaroo paw)	**	**	**	*	***	***	***	***	**	**	**	**	Some varieties not available mid-Spring
Anthuriums	***	***	***	***	***	***	***	***	***	***	***	***	Most colours available throughout the year
Antirrhinum majus	***	***	*	***	***	***	***	***	***	***	***	***	Most colours not available in early Spring
Asclepias	**	***	**	**	**	***	***	***	***	***	***	***	A. incarnata only available early Autumn
Asters	***	***				***	***	***	***	***	***	***	Some varieties only available late Autumn
Astilbe					*	*	*	***	***	***	***	***	A. 'Whasingthon' only available late Spring
Astrantia								*	*	*	*		
Atriplex	**	**	***	***	***	**			**	**	**	**	
Bouvardia	***	***	***	***	***	***	***	***	***	***	***	***	B. longiflorum not available in Spring
Bupleurum griffithii	***	***	***	***	***	***	***	***	***	***	***	***	
Callistephus (China aster)			*	*	*			***	***	***	***		
Campanula					***	***	***						
Carthamus	**	**	**	**			**	***	***	***	***	***	
Celosia	**	**						***	***	***	***	***	
Centaurea cyanus (cornflower)								***	***	***	***		
Centaurea macrocephala								*	*				
Chamelaucium (waxflower)		**	**	**	**								
Chelone obliqua					**	**		***	***	***			
Chrysanthemum santini	***	***	***	***	***	***	***	***	***	***	***	***	
Chrysanthemum (Indicum gr.)	***	***	***	***	***	***	***	***	***	***	***	***	
Cirsium		**	**	**	**			***	***	***	***	***	
Convallaria majalis (lily-of-the-valley)	**	**	**	**	***	***				**	**	**	
Crocosmia (Montbretia)						***	***	***					
Cyclamen	***	***	***	***	***							***	
Cymbidium orchids	***	***	***	***	***					***	***	***	
Dahlias								***	***	***	***		
Delphinium ajacis (larkspur)	***	***	***	***	***	***	***	***	***	***	***		
Delphinium	**	**	**	**	**	**	**	**	**	**	**	**	
Dendrobium orchids	***	***	***	***	***	***	***	***	***	***	***	***	
Dianthus barbatus (sweet william)	*	*	***	***	***	***	***	***	*	*	*	*	
Dianthus (standard carnation)	***	***	***	***	***	***	***	***	***	***	***	***	
Dianthus (spray carnation)	***	***	***	***	***	***	***	***	***	***	***	***	
Echinops								***	***	***	***		
Eremurus stenophyllus (fox tail lily)					***	***	***	***	*	*			
Eryngium	***	***						***	***	***	***	***	
Eupatorium								***	***	***			
Euphorbia fulgens	***	***	***							***	***	***	
Eustoma russellianum	***	***				***	***	***	***	***	***	***	
Forsythia intermedia			***	***	***	***							
Freesia	***	***	***	***	***	***	***	***	***	***	***	***	
Gerbera	***	***	***	***	***	***	***	***	***	***	***	***	
Gladioli								***	***	***	***	***	

Flower Type	Jan	Feb	Mar	Apr	May	Jun	Jul	Aug	Sep	Oct	Nov	Dec	Special Notes
Gloriosa rothschildiana (glory lily)	***	***	**	***	***	***	***	***	***	***	***	***	
Godetia	***	***		***	***	***	***	***	***	***	***	***	
Gomphrena	**	**						**	***	***	***	***	
Gypsophila	***	***	***	***	***	***	***	***	***	***	***	***	
Helenium								***	***	***	***	**	
Helianthus (sunflower)						***	***	***	***	***	***	**	
Heliconia	***	***	***	***	***	***	**	**	**	***	***	***	
Hippeastrum	***	***	***	***	***	***	***			***	***	***	
Hyacinths		**	***	***	***	***	**						
Hydrangea	**	**	**	**	**		**	**	***	***	***	***	
Hypericum	**	**						**	***	***	***	***	
Iris	***	***	***	***	***	***	***	***	***	***	***	***	
Ixia					*	*							
Kniphofia (red hot pokers)						**	**	**	*	*	*	**	
Lathyrus (sweet peas)		*	*	**	***	***	***						
Leucanthemum	***	***	***	***	***	***	***	***	***	***			
Liatris	***	***	***	***	***	***	***	***	***	***	***	***	
Lilium	***	***	***	***	***	***	***	***	***	***	***	***	
Limonium (stratice)	***	***	***	***	***	***	***	***	***	***	***	***	
Lysimachia clethroides			***	***	***	***	***	***	***	***	***	***	
Lysimachia vulgaris	**	**							***	***	**	**	
Matthiola incana (stocks)	*	*	*	*	*				**	**	**	*	*A white variety is available all year*
Mentha (flowering mint)									***	***	***		
Molucella laevis (bells of Ireland)	***	***	***	***	***	***	***	***	***	***	***	***	
Muscari (grape hyacinth)	**	***	***	***	***	***	**					**	
Narcissi		***	***	***	***								
Nerine	***	***	***	***	***	***	***	***	***	***	***	***	
Oenothera								***					
Oncidium (golden showers orchid)	***	***	***	***	***	***	***	***	***	***	***	***	
Origanum								***	***	***	***	***	
Ornithogalum arabicum (Moroccan chincherinchee)	**	**	***	***	***	***		**	**	**	**		
Ornithagalum thyrsoides (chincherinchee)	***	***	***	***	***				***	***	***	***	
Peonies					***	***	***						
Papaver (poppy seed heads)								***	***	***	***	***	
Paphiopedilum (orchid)	***	***	***	**		**	**	**	**	**	***	***	
Phalaenopsis (orchid)	***	***	***	***	***	***	***	***	***	***	***	***	
Phlox	***	***	***	***	***	***	***	***	***	***	***	***	
Physostegia (obedient plant)								*	*	*			
Protea	***	***	***			**						***	
Prunus	**	***	***	***	***	**							
Ranunculus		**	**	**	***	***	***						
Roses	***	***	***	***	***	***	***	***	***	***	***	***	
Saponaria								***	***	***	***		
Scabious								***	***	***	***		
Scilla (bluebells)			***	***	***								
Sedum spectabile									***	***	***	***	
Solidago	***	***	***	***	***	***	***	***	***	***	***	***	
Strelitzia	***	***	***	***	***	***	***	***	***	***	***	***	
Symphoricarpos (snowberry)									***	***	***	***	
Syringa (lilac)	***	***	***	***	***	**						***	
Tanacetum (feverfew)	***	***	***	***	***	***	***	***	***	***	***	***	
Trachelium	***	***	***	***	***	***	***	***	***	***	***	***	*White Trachelium not available early Spring*
Triteleia (Brodiaea)						***	***	***	***	***	***		
Tulips	**	***	***	***	***	***	**					**	
Veronica	***	***	***	***	***	***	***	***	***	***	***	***	
Viburnum opulus (guelder rose)	**	**	***	***	***	***	**	**					
Zantedeschia aethiopica (arum lily)	**	**	***	***	***	***	***	***	***	***	***	**	
Zantedeschia (calla lily)	***	***	***	***	***	***	***	***	***	***	***	***	
Zinnia									***	***	**		

TULIP ARRANGEMENT

· · ·

MATERIALS

· · ·

50 'Angelique' tulips

· · ·

scissors

· · ·

*watertight container, e.g. small
bucket*

· · ·

basket

*The arrangement is technically
relatively unstructured but, by
repetition of the regular form of
the tulip heads, the overall
visual effect is that of a formal
dome of flowers to be viewed in
the round.*

Sometimes the simple beauty of an arrangement which relies entirely on one type of flower in its own foliage can be breathtaking. This display of Angelique tulips in glorious profusion contains nothing to compete with their soft pastel pink colour and would make a dramatic room centrepiece.

1 Strip the lower leaves from the tulips to prevent them from rotting in the water. Fill the bucket with water and place in the basket.

2 Cut each tulip stem to the correct size and place the stems in the water. Arrange them to start building the display from its lowest circumference upwards.

3 Continue arranging the tulips towards the centre of the display until a full and even domed shape is achieved. The display should be able to be viewed from all sides.

Blue and White Tussie Mussies

· · ·

Small, hand-tied spiralled posies make perfect gifts and, in the right vase, ideal centre decorations for small tables. Both of these displays have delicate flowers massed together. One features Japanese anemones, visually strengthened by black-berries on stems; the other delphiniums supported by rosehip stems.

1 Start with a central flower and add stems of foliage and flowers, turning the posy in your hand to build the design into a spiral.

2 Once all the ingredients have been used, and the bunch is completed, tie firmly at the binding point with twine. Repeat steps one and two for the second tussie mussie.

3 Trim the ends of the flower stems with scissors to achieve a neat edge. Finish both tussie mussies with a ribbon bow.

MATERIALS

· · ·

TUSSIE 1 (on left)

· · ·

blackberries on stems

· · ·

white Japanese anemones

· · ·

1 stem draceana

· · ·

twine

· · ·

ribbon

· · ·

scissors

· · ·

TUSSIE 2 (on right)

· · ·

4-5 stems 'Blue Butterfly' delphinium

· · ·

3 stems rosehips

· · ·

5 small Virginia creeper leaves

· · ·

twine

· · ·

ribbon

· · ·

scissors

Whilst the flowers need to be tightly massed for the best effect, they have relatively large but fragile blooms, so take care not to crush their petals, and tie off firmly but gently.

HEAVILY SCENTED
ARRANGEMENT
· · ·

MATERIALS
· · ·
1 block plastic foam
· · ·
cellophane (plastic wrap)
· · ·
wooden trug
· · ·
scissors
· · ·
20 stems golden privet
· · ·
10 stems tuberose
· · ·
10 stems cream stocks
· · ·
20 stems freesias
· · ·
20 stems mimosa

Mimosa has a substantial main stem with slender offshoots. For greater flexibility, remove the offshoots and discard the heavier main stem.

The flowers used in this display are chosen for their distinctive and delicious scents, which combine to produce a heady perfume guaranteed to silence those who claim that commercially-grown blooms do not have the fragrance of their garden equivalents. It is an ideal arrangement for a hallway or living room where the scent will be most attractive.

The outline of the display is established in golden privet reinforced with waxy tuberose and soft-textured stocks. These provide a cream and yellow backdrop for the focal flowers, pale yellow double-petalled freesias. The whole arrangement is visually co-ordinated by the introduction of the soft green feathery foliage and powdery yellow flowers of mimosa.

1 Firmly wedge a water-soaked block of plastic foam into a cellophane-lined (plastic wrap-lined) trug. Trim the excess cellophane from the edge of the trug. (If the finished arrangement is likely to be moved secure the plastic foam in the trug with florist's adhesive tape.)

2 First ensuring the leaves are stripped from the stem bottoms, insert the golden privet into the foam to build the outline of the arrangement. Because they make small neat holes, the slender stems of golden privet are ideal for arranging in plastic foam.

3 Reinforce the outline of the display with the tuberose and the stocks, arranging them in opposite diagonals.

4 Distribute the freesias throughout the display, using stems with buds to the outside and more open blooms to the centre. Break off the mimosa's offshoots so that a mixture of stem sizes can be arranged through the display which will visually pull everything together.

HYACINTH BULB VASES

· · ·

MATERIALS

· · ·

3 bulb vases

· · ·

2 jam jars

· · ·

4 thin sturdy twigs

· · ·

raffia

· · ·

scissors

· · ·

5 hyacinth bulbs

*There are vases expressly
made for water-growing bulbs
and some of the old-fashioned
types are particularly attractive
– so search your local junk and
antique shops. At the same
time, a simple jam jar, with a
twig frame to support the bulb,
will do the job just as well.
This particular arrangement is
a grouping of both types of
container, which are as
important to the overall success
of the display as the flowers
themselves.*

Bulbs can be grown in water as well as in soil. By employing this technique and with some long-term planning, the commonplace hyacinth has been given a new interest in this display.

1 If you are using bulb vases, simply fill each one with water and place the bulbs on the top with their bases sitting in the water. Top up the water occasionally, taking care not to disturb the roots. Then just wait until the hyacinth bulbs root, grow and flower!

2 The use of a jam jar requires making a square frame to sit on top of the jar. Use thin but sturdy twigs firmly tied together with raffia to form the frame. Trim the stem ends and the raffia when you have established that the frame fits the jar neatly, then position the bulb on the frame with its base in the water.

Spring Napkin Decoration

· · ·

The sophisticated gold and white colour combination used in these elegant and delicate napkin decorations would be perfect for a formal dinner or an important occasion such as a wedding.

In addition to its exquisite scent, the tiny bells of lily-of-the-valley visually harmonize with the pure white of the cyclamen.

MATERIALS

· · ·

napkins

· · ·

*small-leaved ivy
trails (sprigs)*

· · ·

scissors

· · ·

1 pot lily-of-the-valley

· · ·

*1 pot tiny cyclamen (dwarf
Cyclamen persicum)*

· · ·

gold cord

The slender stems of both flowers enable each decoration to be made into a tied sheaf. The splayed stems echo the shape made by the flowers.

1 Fold the napkin into a rectangle, then roll into a cylindrical shape. Wrap an ivy trail (sprig) around the middle of the napkin. Tie the stem firmly in a knot.

2 Take 4–5 stems of lily-of-the-valley, 3 flowers of cyclamen on their stems and 3 cyclamen leaves. Using both flowers, create a small flat-backed sheaf in your hand by spiralling the stems. Place one leaf at the back of the lily-of-the-valley for support and use the other two around the cyclamen flowers to emphasize the focal point. Tie at the binding point with gold cord. Lay the flat back of the sheaf on top of the napkin and ivy, wrap the excess gold cord around the napkin, gently tying into a bow on top of the stems.

FRESH HERBAL WREATH
· · ·

MATERIALS

· · ·

*30 cm (12 in) plastic foam
wreath frame*

· · ·

scissors

· · ·

2 branches bay leaves

· · ·

2 bunches rosemary

· · ·

.71 wires

· · ·

6 large bulbs (heads) garlic

· · ·

6 or 7 beetroot (beets)

· · ·

*40 stems flowering
marjoram*

· · ·

40 stems flowering mint

*As well as being decorative, a
herb wreath can also be useful.
The herbs can be taken from it
and used in the kitchen
without causing too much
damage to the overall design.*

I n many parts of Europe it is believed that a herb wreath hung in
a kitchen, or by the entrance of a house, is a sign of welcome,
wealth and good luck. This wreath will stay fresh for two or three
weeks because the stems of the herbs are in water, but even if it
dries out it will continue to look good for some time.

1 Soak the wreath frame
thoroughly in cold
water. Create the
background by making a
foliage outline using evenly
distributed bay leaves and
sprigs of rosemary. To
ensure an even covering,
position the leaves inside,
on top and on the outside
of the wreath frame.

2 Wire the garlic bulbs
(heads) and beetroot
(beets) by pushing two
wires through their base so
that they cross, then pull
the projecting wires down
and cut to the correct
length for the depth of the
foam. Decide where on
the wreath they are to be
positioned and push the
wires firmly into the foam.

3 Infill the spaces in the wreath, concentrating the marjoram around
the beetroot and the mint around the garlic.

SPRING BLOSSOM URN

· · ·

MATERIALS

· · ·

urn

· · ·

cellophane (plastic wrap)

· · ·

1 block plastic foam

· · ·

scissors

· · ·

.71 wires

· · ·

reindeer moss

· · ·

15 stems pussy willow

· · ·

10 stems white lilac

· · ·

*15 stems pink cherry
blossom*

*The bright, fresh arrangement
joyously leaping out of a cold,
hard, metal urn, symbolizes
the winter soil erupting with
spring growth.*

The explosion of plant life in the spring is visually depicted in this arrangement of early flowers and foliage.

Heavily flowered heads of white lilac are the focal blossoms of the display set against the dark brown stems of pussy willow and cherry. The starkness of these stems is softened by the emerging pink blossom of the cherry and the furry silver pussy willow buds, both of which harmonize with the lilac.

1 Line the urn with cellophane (plastic wrap) and wedge in the water-soaked block of plastic foam. Trim away the excess cellophane.

2 Make hairpins from .71 wires and pin reindeer moss into the plastic foam around the rim of the urn. Make sure that the foam is entirely covered on all sides.

3 Arrange the pussy willow in the urn to establish the height and width of a symmetrical outline. Press the pussy willow stems firmly into the plastic foam to secure the arrangement.

4 Distribute the lilac throughout the pussy willow. Look carefully at the way lilac flowers hang from their stems and try to exploit their natural attitude in the arrangement. You will find there is no need to position the stems at extreme angles.

5 Position the pink cherry blossom throughout the display to reinforce the overall shape and provide a link between the slender stems of pussy willow and the large heads of the flowering lilac.

HYACINTH BULB BOWL
. . .

MATERIALS
. . .
8 sprouting hyacinth bulbs
. . .
24 autumn leaves
. . .
raffia
. . .
scissors
. . .
glass bowl

This novel approach to the display of developing hyacinth bulbs takes them out of their pots and into organic containers which become feature elements in the design. This attractive display will last for many weeks.

The bulbs' roots, along with their soil, are simply wrapped in leaves and then grouped together sitting in water in a glass bowl. The bulbs take up the water and happily grow from these attractive green spikes through to full flowers.

1 Carefully remove the hyacinth bulbs from their pots, keeping the soil tightly packed around the roots. Wrap a leaf underneath the root ball and soil of each bulb, with two more leaves around the sides. Leave the majority of each bulb exposed as it would be in a pot.

2 Secure the leaves in position by tying around with raffia. Group the wrapped hyacinths in the glass bowl and fill to approximately 5 cm (2 in) deep with water. Remember to top up regularly. The bulbs will continue to grow and eventually bloom.

NAPKIN TIE

. . .

This beautiful alternative to a napkin ring is easy to make and very effective in enhancing the look of your dinner table. Its appearance can be changed to suit many different occasions.

MATERIALS
. . .
napkin
. . .
scissors
. . .
*long, thin, flexible stem
rosemary*
. . .
3 lemon geranium leaves
. . .
2 or 3 heads flowering mint

1 Find a suitable length of rosemary, long and flexible enough to wrap around the rolled napkin once or twice. Tie the stem securely.

2 Arrange the lemon geranium leaves and mint flowerheads by gently pushing the stems through the knot of the binding rosemary stem.

The method is simply to use any reasonably sturdy trailing foliage to bind the napkin and then create a focal point by the addition of leaves, berries or flowerheads of your choice. If a firm fixing is required, wire the leaves and flowerheads before attaching to binding material.

TULIP POMANDER

. . .

*The pomander illustrated does
not boast exotic aromas but it
does have a pleasing variety of
surface textures, ranging from
the spiky inner petals of double
tulips through the beady black
berries of myrtle to the softness
of grey moss, all set against
bands of smooth satin ribbon.*

In Elizabethan times pomanders were filled with herbs or scented flowers and carried to perfume the air. Today the pomander is more likely to be a bridesmaid's accessory, a charming alternative to the conventional posy.

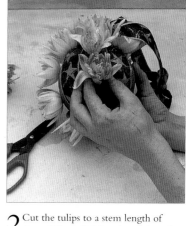

1 Soak the foam ball in water. Tie the ribbon around the ball, starting at the top and crossing at the bottom, and then tying at the top to divide the ball into four equal segments. Make sure there is enough excess ribbon to tie into a bow.

2 Cut the tulips to a stem length of about 2.5 cm (1 in) and push into the foam in vertical lines at the centre of each segment. Hold the tulip heads gently while positioning them on the foam ball to avoid the heads breaking off.

3 Cut sprigs of myrtle on short stems and push into the foam to form lines on either side of each line of tulips. The myrtle should appear quite compact.

4 Form hairpins from the .71 wires and use them to pin the reindeer moss to cover all remaining exposed areas of the foam ball.

AMARYLLIS LINE ARRANGEMENT

• • •

MATERIALS

• • •

pinholder

• • •

shallow bowl

• • •

scissors

• • •

5 stems amaryllis

• • •

6 Phormium cookiannum
variagatum *leaves*

• • •

glass marbles

*The amaryllis has an
extraordinary-looking stem
which, though hollow, is large
and fleshy and carries heavy
blooms. Plastic foam will not
support a flower of this size
and weight unless used in large
amounts, reinforced with wire
mesh with the amaryllis stem
firmly staked.*

*The pinholder will give the
amaryllis the secure support it
requires because the fleshy
stems can be pushed firmly on
to the pins. Furthermore, the
weight of the pinholder is
sufficient to counterbalance the
weight of the blooms.*

A line arrangement is just that: a display of flowers in a staggered vertical line. The large blooms of the amaryllis are particularly suitable and here they are reinforced by the spiky leaves of *Phormium cookiannum variagatum.*

1 Place the pinholder in the centre of the bowl and completely cover it with water. Arrange the amaryllis in a staggered vertical line by pushing the stems on to the pins. Position the more closed blooms on longer stems towards the rear, and more open blooms with shorter stems towards the front of the arrangement. (Any spare flowerheads on short stems should be recessed into the base of the display by securing them on pins.)

2 Arrange the leaves, with the largest at the back and shortest to the front, in a diagonal through the staggered vertical line of amaryllis.

3 To complete the display, place it in its final position and conceal the top of the pinholder by scattering glass marbles on top of it.

NOSEGAYS
· · ·

Popular in Elizabethan times for warding off unpleasant smells, today nosegays, or tussie mussies, still make charming decorations and lovely gifts. The instructions are for the posy on the right of the main picture.

MATERIALS
· · ·
1 chive flower
· · ·
flowering mint
· · ·
rosemary
· · ·
fennel
· · ·
lemon geranium leaves
· · ·
twine
· · ·
scissors
· · ·
raffia

1 Cut all the plant stems to a length suitable for the size of posy you are making and clean them of leaves and thorns. Starting by holding the central flowers in your hand, add stems of the chosen herb, turning the emerging bunch as you work. Make sure you complete a circle with one herb before you start another. Finally use a circle of lemon geranium leaves to edge the bunch.

2 When everything is in position, tie with twine and trim stem ends neatly. Finish each nosegay with raffia tied in a bow.

These tiny herbal posies are made up of tight concentric circles of herbs around a central flower, which will exude a marvellous mix of scents and can be used for culinary as well as decorative purposes. Alternatively they can be left to dry, to provide lasting pleasure.

FRUIT AND FLOWER SWAG

. . .

.71 wires

· · ·

4 limes

· · ·

9 lemons

· · ·

4 bunches black grapes

· · ·

*4 bunches sneezeweed
(Helenium)*

· · ·

1 bundle tree ivy

· · ·

scissors

· · ·

*straw plait (braid), about
60 cm (24 in) long*

· · ·

raffia

· · ·

1 bunch ivy trails (sprigs)

*The component parts have to
be wired, but otherwise the
swag is simple to construct. Do
remember that although lemons
and limes will survive in this
situation, grapes and cut
flowers will need regular mist
spraying with water.*

The colour and content of this decorative swag will brighten any room. Its visual freshness makes it especially suitable for a kitchen but, if it was made on a longer base, the decoration could be a mantelpiece garland or even extended to adorn the balustrade of a staircase.

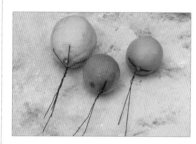

1 First, all the fruit has to be wired. Pass a wire through from side to side just above the base of the limes. Leave equal lengths of wire projecting from either side, bend these down and twist together under the base. If the lemons are heavier than the limes, pass a second wire through at right angles to the first, providing four equal ends to be twisted together under their bases.

2 Group the grapes in small clusters and double leg mount with .71 wires. Then form 12 small bunches of sneezeweed mixed with tree ivy and double leg mount these on .71 wires.

3 Starting at its bottom end, bind three wired lemons to the plait (braid) with raffia. Then in turn bind a bunch of flowers and foliage, a lime, grapes and a second bunch of flowers and foliage.

4 Repeat binding materials to the plait in the above sequence until almost at the top. Secure by wrapping the remaining raffia tightly around the plait.

5 Make a bow from raffia and tie to the top of the swag. Trim off any stray wire ends. Entwine the ivy trails (sprigs) around the top of the swag and bow.

PINK PHLOX ARRANGEMENT
IN A PITCHER

• • •

A simple-to-arrange pitcher of
flowers and foliage becomes an
explosion of colour and scent.

The colour collision between a mass of pink phlox flowerheads and the vibrant autumn reds of Virginia creeper gives this arrangement its visual impact and is a simple, yet effective arrangement to create.

1 Cut the stems of phlox to a length proportionate to the container. Arrange the phlox evenly with taller stems towards the back of the pitcher.

2 Place the cut ends of Virginia creeper trails (sprigs) in the pitcher of water and weave them through the heads of phlox, spreading them out evenly.

CANDLE RING

· · ·

This pretty little candle ring is created on a very small diameter plastic foam ring. Filled with a heady combination of fennel, rosemary, lemon geranium, hyssop and violas, it would be perfect for an intimate dinner table.

MATERIALS

· · ·

15 cm (6 in) diameter plastic
foam ring

· · ·

candlestick

· · ·

scissors

· · ·

small quantities of rosemary,
lemon geranium leaves, fennel,
hyssop and violas

The floral ring is simply placed over the candlestick to create this simple but effective decoration. Never leave a burning candle unattended and do not allow it to burn down to within less than 5 cm (2 in) of the foliage.

1 Soak the plastic foam ring in cold water and place it over the candlestick. Start the arrangement by making a basic outline in the plastic foam with stems of rosemary and geranium leaves, positioning them evenly around the ring. Try to arrange the leaves at different angles to produce a fuller effect.

2 Infill the gaps evenly with the fennel and hyssop, finally add a few violas for colour.

EXOTIC FLOWER
ARRANGEMENT
• • •

The apparent delicacy of some of the flowers in this spectacular arrangement belies their robust nature. Commercially-produced exotic cut flowers not only look fabulous but also have a long life span.

1 Three-quarter fill the fish bowl with cold water. Cut the contorted willow stems to about three times the height of the vase and arrange to form the framework of the display.

2 Add the ginger flowers and lotus seedheads so that the tallest is slightly shorter than the contorted willow and placed at the back, with stems of decreasing height positioned to the front and sides.

3 Distribute the celosias through the display in the same way as the ginger flowers and lotus heads. Recess the two pink pineapples in the centre of the arrangement, leaving one taller than the other.

Most of the flowers and foliage in this display can subsequently be dried.

4 Position the glory lilies through the arrangement concentrating on the front and sides where they will naturally overhang the container. Arrange the anthuriums, which are the focal flowers, with tallest to the back becoming shorter to the front.

5 Untypically the foliage is added last. Distribute the individual exotic leaves and bunches of bear grass throughout the arrangement. Push the cut ends of the passion flower trails (sprays) into the back of the fish bowl and drape them down and around over the front.

ORCHID POSY

· · ·

MATERIALS

· · ·

*6 stems orange/brown spotted
spray orchid*

· · ·

*6 stems pink spotted spray
orchid*

· · ·

bear grass

· · ·

scissors

· · ·

twine

*This tied posy is spiralled in
the hand and contains just two
varieties of orchid with fronds
of bear grass. The strong stems
of orchids are ideal for the
spiralling technique and allow
the finished posy to stand on
its own and still keep its
shape. The elegance of the bear
grass helps the overall design
by softening the solid outlines
of the fleshy flowerheads.*

The orchid grows in a multiplicity of shapes and colours, from delicate spray forms to large fleshy varieties. All orchids look exotic and can easily upstage other more subtle blooms in an arrangement. It follows that the orchid is most effective when used on its own in a single variety, or perhaps with other compatible varieties and some carefully chosen foliage.

1 Starting with a central orchid stem held in your hand, add flower stems and foliage to form a spiral. Separate the bear grass into slim bunches for easy handling.

2 Keep turning the posy in your hand as you add the stems, not forgetting to include the bunches of bear grass, until the arrangement is complete. Trim the stems.

3 Using the twine, tie the finished bunch at the binding point – i.e. where all the stems cross. Finish the posy by tying bear grass around the binding point to conceal the twine.

EXOTIC BUD VASE
. . .

A selection of small colourful vases forms the basis of this attractive display of short-stemmed exotic flowers. Only one type of flower is used for each jar. Some have a single stem with a particular sculptural quality; others have flowers massed for colour and texture impact. It is a simple, effective display which relies as much on the choice of containers as the flowers used.

MATERIALS
. . .
1 anthurium
. . .
1 pink pineapple
. . .
contorted willow stems
. . .
3 exotic leaves
. . .
3 celosia heads
. . .
3 stems spray orchid
. . .
4 glory lily heads
. . .
*10 Scarborough lily
flowers*
. . .
*6 small different coloured
ceramic containers*
. . .
scissors

Sometimes we are left with flowers on stems which are too short for large arrangements. Perhaps they are flowers salvaged from fading displays which have been cut shorter to extend their lives or perhaps they are simply broken stems. Nevertheless, they can still be used to good effect.

1 Consider the shape, size, colour and texture of the materials and containers to decide which flowers are appropriate to which container. Also decide whether to use a single flowerhead, or a group display for each container.

2 Measure the flower stem lengths against their container. Anthurium is a single display, as is the pineapple but with willow and exotic leaves. The celosia, orchids, glory lily and Scarborough lily are all used to create a massed effect.

ALL-FOLIAGE ARRANGEMENT

. . .

MATERIALS

. . .

2 blocks plastic foam

. . .

*shallow bowl large enough for
the plastic foam blocks*

. . .

florist's adhesive tape

. . .

scissors

. . .

.71 wires

. . .

bun moss

. . .

5 stems grevillea

. . .

*10 stems shrimp plant
(Beloperone guttata)*

. . .

*10 stems ming fern
(cultivar of Boston fern)*

. . .

10 stems pittosporum

. . .

5 stems cotoneaster

*Do not restrict yourself to
green foliage; remember the
bright yellow of elaeagnus, the
silver grey of senecio, not to
mention the extraordinary
autumn wealth of coloured
berries and leaves – all can be
used to achieve truly
wonderful results.*

If the garden is void of flowers, your budget is limited, or you simply fancy a change, then creating an arrangement entirely from different types of foliage can be both challenging and rewarding.

No matter what the season, finding three or four varieties of foliage is not difficult. Anything from the common privet to the most exotic shrubs can be used and to great effect.

1 Soak the plastic foam and secure it in the bowl with florist's adhesive tape.

2 Make hairpin shapes from .71 wire and pin clumps of bun moss around the rim of the bowl by pushing the wires through the moss into the plastic foam. This conceals the plastic foam where it meets the edge of the bowl.

3 Start arranging the grevillea from one side, to establish the maximum height, and work diagonally across with progressively shorter stems, finishing with foliage flowing over the front of the bowl. Arrange the shrimp plant in a similar way along the opposite diagonal, but make it shorter than the grevillea and emphasize this line by adding ming fern.

4 Strengthen the line of grevillea by interspersing it with the broader-leafed pittosporum. Finally, distribute the cotoneaster evenly throughout the whole arrangement.

GERBERA BOTTLE DISPLAY
· · ·

*Gerberas have soft flexible
stems which tend to bend
naturally. To straighten them,
wrap together the top three
quarters of their stems in paper
to keep them erect. Then stand
them in deep cool water for
approximately two hours.*

The success of a display of flowers need not rely on its complexity; indeed it is held by many that simplicity is the essence of good design.

The flowers of the gerbera have an extraordinary visual innocence and a vast array of vibrant colours. This powerful graphic quality makes the gerbera perfect for simple, bold, modern designs which this arrangement demonstrates by isolating blooms in separate containers within an overall grouping. The impact is perpetuated in the water by the addition of food colouring.

1 Add the red and yellow food colourings separately to water and mix thoroughly together. Fill the various bottles or vases. For maximum impact, choose different shapes and sizes of bottles and vary the strength of food colouring to each vessel. The food colouring will not harm the flowers in any way.

2 Measure the gerbera stems to the desired height and cut them at an angle. Place them in bottles individually or in twos and threes, depending on the size of the bottle neck. Finally, arrange the bottles in an eye-catching group, using other colourful props if desired.

GROWING PLANTS TABLE DECORATION

· · ·

It is possible to avoid the time-consuming preparation which is a necessary part of flower arranging by using potted plants. A table decoration need not be the traditional arrangement of cut flowers. An interesting selection of contrasting small plants of different heights has been used in this display. Their status has been elevated by planting them in old terracotta pots of different sizes to give variation to the height of the decoration.

To tie the display together visually, the pots are grouped with interspersed coloured night-lights (tea-lights), each sitting on a leaf which is not only decorative, but will also catch the dripping wax.

MATERIALS

· · ·

2 violas

· · ·

2 ornamental cabbages

· · ·

1 African violet

· · ·

1 cyclamen

· · ·

6 small terracotta pots of different sizes

· · ·

bun moss

· · ·

night-lights (tea-lights)

· · ·

large leaves

1 Remove all the plants from their plastic containers, plant them in terracotta pots, and then water well. Cover the top of the soil in the pots with fresh, moist bun moss. Be sure to allow the pots to drain thoroughly. Arrange the pots at the centre of the table and intersperse with night-lights (tea-lights) placed on leaves, large enough to be visible and to catch the dripping wax.

The group can be as large or small as the table size dictates and the plants can be used around the house between dinner parties.
Never leave burning candles unattended and do not allow them to burn down to within 5cm (2in) of the display.

APRICOT ROSE AND PUMPKIN
· · ·

MATERIALS
· · ·

1 block plastic foam
· · ·
knife
· · ·
marble bird bath, or similar container
· · ·
florist's adhesive tape
· · ·
scissors
· · ·
10 stems hypericum
· · ·
5 tiny pumpkins
· · ·
.71 wires
· · ·
10 stems apricot spray roses

The simple appeal of this design results from its use of just one type of flower and one type of foliage. The addition of tiny pumpkins gives body to the pretty combination of spray roses and flowering hypericum foliage. Note how the apricot colour is carried through the flowers, pumpkins and container in contrast to the red buds and yellow flowers of the foliage.

1 Soak the block of plastic foam and cut it so that it can be wedged in place in the container. Secure the foam with florist's adhesive tape .

2 Create the outline of the display using the hypericum and establish its overall height, width and length. The stems of commercially-produced hypericum tend to be long and straight with many offshoots of smaller stems. To create a more delicate foliage effect, and to get the most out of your material, use these smaller stems in the arrangement.

3 Wire each pumpkin by pushing one wire right through across the pumpkin base and out of the other side. Push another wire through to cross the first at right angles. Pull both wires down so that they project from the base. The pumpkins will be supported by pushing these wires into the plastic foam.

4 Position the pumpkins in the foliage, making sure that some are recessed more than others.

5 Infill the arrangement with the spray roses. Like the hypericum, spray roses tend to have lots of small offshoots from the main stem and these should be used to get the most out of your materials. To augment the overall shape of the display, use buds on longer stems at the outside edges with the most open blooms and heavily-flowered stems in the centre.

Substituting limes for the pumpkins will add a touch of vibrancy but for a more sophisticated look, use plums or black grapes.

Exotic Napkin Decoration
. . .

Materials

. . .
napkin
. . .
*trails (sprays) passion
flower*
. . .
scissors
. . .
*2-3 virginia creeper
leaves*
. . .
1 glory lily head
. . .
1 celosia head

*Exotic flowers are surprisingly
robust, so you can prepare the
napkin decorations in advance
of your dinner party and they
will not droop.*

W hen Oriental food is on the menu, this easy-to-make napkin decoration
will give the dining table the perfect finishing touch.

Passion flower trails (sprays) are bound around the napkin and tied off in a knot
into which the flowerheads and leaves are pushed to hold them in place.

1 Fold the napkin into a rectangle and
then loosely roll up. Wrap a passion
flower trail (spray) around its middle,
pulling quite tightly but taking care not to
snap it, then tie off in a simple knot.

2 Using the virginia creeper leaves, start
arranging the decoration on the
napkin by carefully pushing the stems
through the knot, then repeat the process
with the flowerheads.

HERBAL TABLE DECORATION

This table decoration is made up of five elements: four terracotta pots of various herbs, foliages contained within a plastic foam ring, night-lights (tea-lights) and white dill. This is an interesting alternative to the more conventional concept of an arrangement held in plastic foam, or wire mesh, in a single container.

1 Press the night-lights (tea-lights) into the soaked plastic foam ring, at equal distances around its circumference. Soak the block of plastic foam and line the terracotta pots with cellophane to prevent leakage. Cut the plastic foam to size and fit it firmly into the pots.

2 Mass the white dill around the base ring between the night-lights (tea-lights). Then mass the individual pots with selected herbs and foliage. The effect is greater if each pot is filled with one type of herb only. Position the base ring and arrange the pots within it.

MATERIALS

. . .

6 night-lights (tea-lights)

. . .

30 cm (12 in) diameter plastic foam wreath frame

. . .

2 blocks plastic foam

. . .

4 terracotta pots

. . .

cellophane (plastic wrap)

. . .

scissors

. . .

white dill

. . .

rosemary

. . .

mint

. . .

marjoram

. . .

guelder rose
(Viburnum opulus)
(European cranberry) berries

This display can be dismantled and the parts used separately to good effect in different situations. The individual terracotta pots of herbs can even be dried and their usefulness extended. Never leave burning candles unattended.

TABLE ARRANGEMENT WITH FRUIT AND FLOWERS

· · ·

MATERIALS
· · ·
basket
· · ·
cellophane (plastic wrap)
· · ·
2 blocks plastic foam
· · ·
scissors
· · ·
florist's adhesive tape
· · ·
1 bundle tree ivy
· · ·
3 bunches red grapes
· · ·
.71 wires
· · ·
6 black figs
· · ·
15 stems antirrhinum
· · ·
15 stems amaranthus (straight, not trailing)
· · ·
15 stems astilbe
· · ·
20 stems red roses
· · ·
5 stems hydrangea

The addition of fruit brings a visual opulence to this arrangement of flowers. The sumptuous reds and purples of the figs and grapes used in this display harmonize beautifully with the rich deep hues of the flowers. The natural bloom on the fruit combines with the velvet softness of the roses to create a textural feast for the eye. The overall effect is one of ravishing lusciousness.

1 Line the basket with cellophane (plastic wrap) and tightly wedge in the blocks of water-soaked plastic foam. Trim the excess cellophane around the edge of the basket. If the arrangement is to be moved, tape the foam firmly in place.

2 To establish the overall shape of the arrangement, create a low dome of foliage with the tree ivy in proportion with the size and shape of the basket. Spread the tree ivy evenly throughout the plastic foam.

3 Wire the bunches of grapes by double leg mounting on .71 wires. Position the bunches recessed in the foliage in a roughly diagonal line across the display. Handle the grapes delicately.

4 Push a wire through each fig from side to side, leaving projecting ends to bend downwards. Group the figs in pairs and push the wires into the plastic foam around the centre of the arrangement.

5 Emphasize the domed shape of the display with the antirrhinums, amaranthus and the astilbe. Then add the roses, which are the focal flowers, evenly through the display. To complete the arrangement, recess the hydrangea heads into the plastic foam to give depth and texture. Water the foam daily to prolong the life of the display.

Although there are numerous ingredients in this display, the final effect is well worth the extra attention.

OLD-FASHIONED GARDEN ROSE ARRANGEMENT

· · ·

MATERIALS

· · ·

*watertight container, to put
inside plant pot*

· · ·

*low, weathered terracotta plant
pot*

· · ·

pitcher

· · ·

*a variety of garden roses, short-
and long-stemmed*

· · ·

scissors

*The technique is to mass one
type of flower in several
varieties whose papery petals
will achieve a textural mix of
colour and scent.*

The beautiful full-blown blooms of these antique-looking roses give an opulent and romantic feel to a very simple combination of flower and container. This arrangement deserves centre stage in any room setting.

1 Place the watertight container inside the terracotta plant pot and fill with water. Fill the pitcher as well. Select and prepare your blooms and remove the lower foliage and thorns.

2 Position the longer-stemmed blooms in the pitcher with the heads massed together. This ensures that the cut stems are supported and so can simply be placed directly into the water.

3 Mass shorter, more open flowerheads in the glass bowl inside the plant pot with the stems hidden and the heads showing just above the rim of the pot. The heads look best if kept either all on one level or in a slight dome shape. If fewer flowers are used, wire mesh or plastic foam may be needed to control the positions of individual blooms.

BLUE AND YELLOW
BUD VASES
· · ·

The bud vase is possibly the most common form of table decoration, but that does not mean that it has to be commonplace. These delightful examples, using primary colours, demonstrate that with just a little imagination the simple bud vase can be exciting.

MATERIALS

· · ·

2 bud vases

· · ·

3 stems helenium

· · ·

scissors

· · ·

5 virginia creeper leaves

· · ·

3 stems delphinium

· · ·

2 stems campanula

· · ·

3 small vine leaves

· · ·

raffia

When deciding on a bud vase and its contents, consider both the size of the table and the proportion of flowers to the container used.
Generally bud vases are used on small dining tables and therefore must not be too large and obtrusive. Also a small container with tall flowers is unstable and likely to be knocked over. The water should be changed, or at least topped-up, daily.

1 Fill the vases approximately three-quarters full with water. Measure the stems of your helenium next to your chosen vase in order to achieve the correct height, then cut the stems at an angle and place in the vase. Position virginia creeper leaves around the top of the vase to frame the helenium.

2 Use two or three flowered stems of delphinium and also use the delicate tendrils of buds which are perfect for small arrangements. Prune the relatively large leaves of the campanula before adding. Finally, position the vine leaves around the base of the flowers in the neck of the vase, and finish off each vase with a raffia tie.

SUMMER BASKET DISPLAY

• • •

Summer brings an abundance of varied and beautiful material for the flower arranger. The lovely scents, luscious blooms and vast range of colours available provide endless possibilities for creating wonderful displays.

This arrangement is a bountiful basket, overflowing with seasonal summer blooms which is designed for a large table or sideboard but could be scaled up or down to suit any situation.

MATERIALS

• • •

basket

• • •

cellophane (plastic wrap)

• • •

scissors

• • •

2 blocks plastic foam

• • •

florist's adhesive tape

• • •

*10 stems Viburnum
tinus*

• • •

*15 stems larkspur
in 3 colours*

• • •

*6 lily stems, such as
'Stargazer'*

• • •

5 large ivy leaves

• • •

10 stems white phlox

Keep the display well watered and it should go on flowering for at least a week. The lilies should open fully in plastic foam and new phlox buds will keep opening to replace the spent heads.

1 Line the basket with cellophane (plastic wrap) to prevent leakage, and cut to fit. Then secure the two soaked blocks of plastic foam in the lined basket with the florist's adhesive tape.

2 Arrange the viburnum stems in the plastic foam to establish the overall height, width and shape. Strengthen the outline using the larkspur, making sure you use all of the stems and not just the flower spikes.

3 Place the lilies in a diagonal line across the arrangement. Position the large ivy leaves around the lilies in the centre of the display. Arrange the phlox across the arrangement along the opposite diagonal to the lilies.

EXOTIC TABLE ARRANGEMENT
. . .

wire mesh

. . .

bowl

. . .

*10 croton (Codiaeum)
leaves*

. . .

*10 red Scarborough lily
flowers*

. . .

scissors

. . .

7 Celosia

. . .

7 glory lilies

. . .

.71 wires

. . .

1 mango

*When planning a table
arrangement, choose the
container with care. If the
container is too large it may
obstruct your guests' view
across the dinner table.*

This feast of red flowers and coloured foliage with its touches of yellow and green is bursting with exotic vibrance. The tiny flame-like petals of the glory lily set against the velvet texture of the celosia create a rich display of light and shade, and the bright yellow ceramic container heightens the overall impact. Use it as a focal point for an extravagant party table.

1 Scrunch up the wire mesh and place it in the bottom of the bowl. Fill approximately two-thirds with water. Position the croton leaves by pushing the stems of leaves into the wire mesh for support, creating a framework within which to build the arrangement.

2 Distribute the Scarborough lily flowers throughout the arrangement by pushing the stems into the wire mesh.

3 Cut the cockscomb to between 15 and 20 cm (6 and 8 in) long and ensure that all foliage is removed as this will rot in the water. Distribute evenly throughout the arrangement pushing the stems into the wire mesh.

4 Cut the glory lily flowers to between 15 and 20 cm (6 and 8 in) and push into the arrangement and through the wire mesh. Ensure you have an even spread of flowerheads throughout the arrangement.

5 Push .71 wires into the underside of the mango and cut to between 15 and 20 cm (6 and 8 in). Carefully position the mango off-centre and slightly recessed in the arrangement by pushing the wires through into the wire mesh. Gently part the flowerheads to position the mango to ensure no flowers are damaged in the process. Finally, ensure all stems are in water.

Take care when handling the mango to avoid bruising its delicate skin.

TULIP TOPIARY TREE

· · ·

MATERIALS

· · ·

*1 block plastic foam for dried
flowers*

· · ·

knife

· · ·

basket

· · ·

raffia

· · ·

*5 30 cm (12 in) cinnamon
sticks*

· · ·

scissors

· · ·

glue gun and glue

· · ·

.71 wires

· · ·

reindeer moss

· · ·

*1 plastic foam ball,
approximately 15 cm (6 in)
diameter*

· · ·

open tulip heads

*To get the best result from the
flowerheads, they have been
spread open to reveal their
centres. This not only serves to
increase their visual impact but
also, of course, increases their
surface area which means fewer
blooms are needed.*

The flowers used to make this stunning decorative tree are unlike conventional tulips which have only one layer of petals. These tulips have layer upon layer of different sized petals which together create a very dense, rounded head, reminiscent of a peony.

1 Cut and fit the block of dry plastic foam into the basket base. Depending on its stability, the container may need to be weighted with wet sand, stones, or plaster of Paris, for example. Using the raffia, tie the cinnamon sticks together at both top and bottom and push the resulting tree trunk into the foam to approximately 4 cm (1½ in), securing with glue.

2 Make hairpins out of the .71 wires and with these pin the reindeer moss into the plastic foam in the basket at the base of the tree, completely covering the dry plastic foam.

3 Soak the plastic foam ball in cold water. Carefully apply a small amount of hot glue to the top end of the cinnamon stick trunk and push the wet foam ball approximately 4 cm (1½ in) on to it.

4 Make sure that the flowerheads are as open as possible by holding the flower in your hand and gently spreading the petals back, even to the extent of folding those at the edge completely inside-out.

5 Cut the tulip heads with a stem length of approximately 4 cm (1½ in) and push them into the soaked foam ball, covering the surface evenly. Handle the flowerheads with care to avoid crushing.

LILY AND HYACINTH
PLANTED BASKET

· · ·

*The branches of red-barked
dogwood are tied with raffia to
form a decorative and
supportive structure around the
arrangement. A more formal
look can be achieved by
substituting bamboo canes, tied
perhaps with strips of velvet in
rich colours.*

W̶hen the budget is tight, an economic way of creating a large display with
lots of impact is to use plants instead of cut flowers.

This arrangement in a basket combines two totally different plants, which will
continue to flower for weeks. The lily buds will open in sequence and their scent,
mixed with that of hyacinths, will fill the air with an intoxicating perfume.

1 Line the whole basket with a layer of
moss, then in turn line the moss with
cellophane (plastic wrap) to contain the
moisture. Cut to fit.

2 Using the soil from their pots, plant
the three lilies into the lined basket,
with the hyacinth bulbs between them.
Cover the soil with moss.

3 Push four branches of
dogwood through the
moss and into the soil to
form a square around the
plants. Cross those
horizontally with four
more branches, tying them
together with raffia to
create a frame, then trim
the raffia.

WHITE JAPANESE
ANEMONE VASE
· · ·

This delightful arrangement combining forest fruits and rosehips with garden anemones, though simple in concept, becomes a sumptuous display when placed in this elegant vase.

MATERIALS
· · ·
vase
· · ·
scissors
· · ·
blackberries still on
their stems
· · ·
rosehips on stems
· · ·
white Japanese anemones
'Honorine Jobert')
· · ·
vine leaves

The simplest things can be the most effective but when arranging flowers in water, without the help of plastic foam or wire mesh, it is important to consider very carefully the visual effect of the container on the flowers. The rosehips and blackberry stalks used here are very prickly; they need careful handling and the thorns need to be stripped. However, these stems form a strong framework to hold the delicate anemones in position. The addition of vine leaves around the neck of the vase provides a finishing touch for the arrangement.

1 Having filled the vase with water, use the blackberry stems to establish the outline shape. Add the stems of rosehips to reinforce both the structure and the visual balance of the display.

2 Add the anemones evenly throughout the arrangement. Take great care with anemones as they are extremely delicate.

3 Place the stems of the vine leaves in the water so that they form a collar around the base of the arrangement and are visible above the neck of the vase.

HYDRANGEA BASKET EDGING
· · ·

MATERIALS
· · ·
30 autumn leaves
· · ·
.71 wires
· · ·
scissors
· · ·
30 fresh late hydrangea heads
· · ·
basket
· · ·
.32 silver reel (rose) wire

*Hydrangea heads cut late in
their growing season have
toughened and will not wilt
out of water. These together
with autumn leaves, selected so
that they are pliable enough to
wire, have been used in a floral
decoration which can evolve
from fresh to dry and remain
attractive.*

Take mature hydrangea heads and some autumn leaves, and with a little imagination an old wicker basket is transformed into a delightful container. Whether you fill it with fruit or seasonal pot pourri, this basket will make a decorative and long-lasting addition to your home.

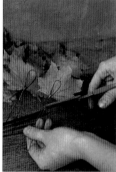

1 Wire the leaves by stitching and double leg mounting on .71 wires.

2 Wire clusters of hydrangea by double leg mounting on .71 wires.

3 Secure the wired hydrangea clusters and leaves alternately around the basket edge by stitching through the gaps in the basket with .32 silver reel (rose) wire. Keep the clusters tightly together to ensure a full edging.

4 When the entire basket edge is covered, finish by stitching the .32 reel wire through several times. If the arrangement is placed in an airy position, the hydrangea heads will dry naturally and prolong the basket's use.

ORNAMENTAL CABBAGE TREE
· · ·

MATERIALS
· · ·

medium-sized terracotta pot

· · ·

cellophane (plastic wrap)

· · ·

sand

· · ·

*1 block plastic foam, for
dried flowers*

· · ·

knife

· · ·

scissors

· · ·

piece of tree root

· · ·

*2 large handfuls sphagnum
moss*

· · ·

twine

· · ·

.71 wires

· · ·

*10 miniature ornamental
cabbages*

*The tree "trunk" is simply a
piece of root, at the top of
which is fixed a moisture-
retaining ball of sphagnum
moss. The cabbage heads are
wired to the moss ball and, by
absorbing water from it and an
occasional mist spraying, will
survive for a week or more.*

O rnamental trees can be created from all sorts of materials for all sorts of decorative uses. This design might be thought unusual in that it uses cabbage
heads to form a "topiary foliage" crown to the tree.

1 Line the medium-sized terracotta pot
with cellophane (plastic wrap) and
approximately half fill with wet sand for
stability. Cut a piece of plastic foam and
wedge it into the pot on top of the sand.
Trim the cellophane if necessary.

2 Push the root into the plastic foam.
Make sure you do this only once as
repeated adjustments will loosen the grip
of the foam and the "trunk" will not be
stable. (Indeed, you could help make it
more secure by placing some glue on the
root base before pushing it into the foam.)
Form a generous handful of sphagnum
moss into a dense ball by criss-crossing it
around with twine.

3 Push the moss ball on to the top of
the root and secure it by threading
wires horizontally through it, leaving the
projecting ends to pull down and wrap
around the "trunk".

4 Using .71 wires, double leg mount the
miniature ornamental cabbage heads
and individually stitch wire any loose
cabbage leaves.

5 Push the wires projecting from the cabbage heads into the moss ball to cover it completely. Fill any gaps with the individual leaves.

6 Make hairpin shapes from .71 wires to fix sphagnum moss to the plastic foam at the base of the tree making sure it is completely covered.

SUNFLOWER PINHOLDER
DISPLAY
• • •

MATERIALS
· · ·
low ceramic dish
· · ·
pinholder
· · ·
scissors
· · ·
*3-5 stems contorted hazel
twigs*
· · ·
9 stems sunflowers
· · ·
5 large ivy leaves

*The pinholder enables the
flower arranger to create
beautiful and simple designs
without the need for a large
container.
The pinholder is weighted so
that even the top-heavy
sunflowers in this arrangement
are totally stable once their
stems are pushed onto the
metal pins.*

This pinholder display results in an informal and minimalist grouping whose glorious sunflowers, set against a backdrop of contorted hazel, shine out undiminished by the clutter of other flowers.

1 Fill the dish with sufficient water to cover the pinholder. Cut the stems of hazel and push them on to the pins to create a tall outline shape.

2 Position the sunflowers, pushing the cut stems on to the pins. Grade the flowers according to the size of their heads. The smallest heads should be on the tallest stems at the top of the arrangement, with the larger heads on shorter stems towards the focal point. Create a staggered line of blooms from top to bottom. Recess a couple of flowerheads and bring the line of flowers over the front of the container to one side, following the outline formed by the contorted hazel.

3 Position the ivy leaves around the focal flower at the centre and add others low down in the display. The leaves will help give visual depth and their dark, green colour will be a suitable background for the bright yellow of the flowers.

Yellow Calla Lily Arrangement

. . .

This display highlights the striking beauty of the calla lily. It ingeniously exploits the visual power of the almost luminescent golden-yellow blooms of this flower by setting them against a carefully controlled background of blue and green accompanying material.

The chincherinchees have cool green stems and creamy white flowerheads with beady black centres which give interest as well as height to the arrangement.

The viburnum is used as a framework for the display and its metallic blue berries provide a visual bridge between the two flowers it accompanies.

MATERIALS

. . .

shallow dish

. . .

pinholder

. . .

scissors

. . .

10 stems viburnum berries

. . .

11 stems Moroccan chincherinchee (Ornithogalum arabicum)

. . .

5 stems yellow calla lily

The whole arrangement is mounted on a pinholder which becomes almost invisible, so avoiding the distraction of a container.

1 Fill the shallow dish with sufficient water to cover the pinholder when placed within it. Arrange the viburnum by pushing the cut stem ends down onto the pins and use this foliage to create the outline shape of the display and establish its height and width.

2 Arrange the chincherinchees on the pins to run diagonally through the viburnum foliage outline, varying the stem heights.

3 Arrange the calla lilies on the pins. Roughly follow an "S" shape, with the smallest bloom on the longest stem at the back, working forwards and down with larger blooms on shorter stems.

AUTUMN CROCUS TRUG

· · ·

MATERIALS

· · ·

trug

· · ·

cellophane (plastic wrap)

· · ·

6 flowering crocus bulbs

· · ·

bun moss

· · ·

autumn leaves

· · ·

raffia

· · ·

scissors

Although one expects to see crocuses in the spring, this beautiful autumn variety is a welcome sight as its flowers push up determinedly through the fallen leaves. Of course, they do not have to be confined to the garden.

Bring the outdoors inside by planting up an old trug with flowering crocus bulbs in soil covered in a natural-looking carpet of moss and leaves. This simple display is as effective as the most sophisticated cut-flower arrangement.

1 Line the trug with cellophane (plastic wrap) and plant the bulbs in soil.

2 Ensure the bulbs are firmly planted and watered. Arrange the bun moss on top of the soil, then scatter the leaves over the moss to create an autumnal effect.

3 Tie raffia into bows, one on either side of the base of the trug handle.

AUTUMN CANDLE DISPLAY
· · ·

MATERIALS
· · ·
1 block plastic foam
· · ·
1 metal candleholder
· · ·
6 crab apples
· · ·
1 small pumpkin
· · ·
*3 Chinese lantern
heads*
· · ·
.71 wires, .38 wires
· · ·
scissors
· · ·
hypericum buds
· · ·
2 stems spray roses
· · ·
1 beeswax candle

*Beeswax candles have an
attractive texture and natural
honey colouring which are the
perfect accompaniment for this
seasonal rustic display.*

The autumn fruits of Chinese lanterns, crab apples and baby pumpkins are put to good use in this charming and compact candle decoration. The natural rich colouring of the fruits and the deep red of the hypericum buds complement beautifully the soft apricot tones of the spray roses.

1 Soak the plastic foam in water and cut it into small pieces to fit into the candleholder drip tray. Firmly wedge into the drip tray to support the arrangement.

2 Wire the crab apples and pumpkin on .71 wires and Chinese lantern heads on .38 wires. All wires should be cut to approximately 4 cm (1½ in) in length.

3 By pushing wires into the foam, position the pumpkin, 2 groups of 3 crab apples and a group of 3 Chinese lantern heads, spacing them equally around the circumference of the drip tray.

4 Arrange the hypericum foliage between the fruits by pushing short stems into the plastic foam to create the outline shape of the display.

5 Cut flowerheads from the spray roses on stems long enough to push into the plastic foam amongst the foliage and fruits. Use rose buds towards the outside edge of the arrangement, and more open blooms towards the centre. Remember to ensure that there is enough space left to accommodate the beeswax candle.

Never leave burning candles unattended and do not allow them to burn down to within 5 cm (2 in) of the display height.

BLUE AND YELLOW
ARRANGEMENT IN A PITCHER
· · ·

MATERIALS
· · ·

10 stems 'Blue Butterfly'
delphinium
· · ·

2 bunches sneezeweed
(Helenium)
· · ·

3 stems dracaena
· · ·

raffia
· · ·

scissors
· · ·

pitcher

*The choice of container is
important since it becomes a
major element in the design.
The yellow pitcher gives the
display a country look, but of
course the same arrangement
would look more sophisticated
if the container was a
contemporary glass vase.*

The sunny yellow faces of sneezeweed become almost luminous when set against the electric blue colour of 'Blue Butterfly' delphinium, a brave colour combination guaranteed to brighten any situation. The easy-to-make, hand-tied spiral bunch is designed to look as though the flowers have just been cut and loosely arranged.

1 Lay out the materials for ease of working. Build the display by alternately adding stems of different material while continuously turning the growing bunch in your hand so that the stems form a spiral.

2 Continue the process until all materials are used and you have a full display of flowers. At the binding point, i.e. where all the stems cross, tie firmly with raffia. Trim the stem ends to the length dictated by the container.

LARGE DAHLIA ARRANGEMENT

· · ·

Dahlias bloom vigorously all through the summer and until the first frosts of autumn, offering dazzling variations of colour and shape for the flower arranger. The complex and precise geometry of the dahlia flowerheads ensures that, even with the informality of the bright red rosehips and softness of the campanulas, the arrangement retains a structured feel.

MATERIALS

· · ·

large, watertight pot

· · ·

15 stems campanula

· · ·

scissors

· · ·

10 stems long-stemmed
rosehips

· · ·

30 stems pompom dahlias

These beautiful golden dahlias have clean, long straight stems which makes them easy to arrange in a large display. They would also survive well in plastic foam.

1 Fill the pot three-quarters full with water. Create the basic domed outline and the structure using the leafy campanula.

2 Cut and strip the thorns from the stems of the rosehips and arrange in amongst the campanula, varying the heights as required to follow the domed outline.

3 Cut the pompom dahlias to the required heights and add to the arrangement, distributing them evenly throughout. The aim is to achieve a smooth domed effect.

MANTELPIECE ARRANGEMENT
· · ·

MATERIALS
· · ·

1 block plastic foam

· · ·

plastic tray for plastic foam

· · ·

florist's adhesive tape

· · ·

scissors

· · ·

5 stems birch twigs

· · ·

6 stems Butcher's broom
(Ruscus)

· · ·

5 stems Eupohorbia
fulgens

· · ·

7 stems straight amaranthus

· · ·

5 stems spray chrysanthemums

· · ·

5 stems alstroemeria

· · ·

7 stems eustoma

*On its own, or combined with
a fireplace arrangement
(pictured opposite and featured
over the page), this mantelpiece
arrangement creates a stunning
focal point to a room.*

The mantelpiece offers a prominent position for a floral display. The challenge is to create not just a visual balance, but a physical balance too. The mantel shelf is relatively narrow and flowers must be carefully positioned to avoid them toppling forwards. So, as you build, ensure stability by keeping the weight at the back and as near the bottom of the display as is practical.

The delicate stems of ruscus and euphorbia fulgens are lightweight in relation to their length and thus ideal for this type of arrangement. Their natural trailing habit means they can be positioned to give width along the shelf and length over its front edge and, together with birch twigs, they give the display its structure. The addition of a selection of strongly coloured flowers brings the arrangement vibrantly alive.

1 Soak the block of plastic foam in cold water and securely tape into the plastic tray with florist's adhesive tape. Position the tray at the centre of the mantelpiece.

2 Arrange the birch twigs and ruscus in the plastic foam to establish height and width. Take advantage of the natural curving habit of the ruscus to trail over the container.

3 Add the scarlet plume to emphasize the trailing nature of the display. Distribute the amaranthus throughout the display to reinforce the established shape.

4 The spray chrysanthemums are the focal flowers and should be roughly staggered to either side of the vertical axis at the centre of the display. The alstroemeria stems add strength and, by recessing one or two of them, depth to the arrangement.

5 A stem of good quality eustoma has two to three side stems. Split these off to make the most of the flowers. Use budded stems towards the outside of the display and more open blooms towards its centre, making sure some are recessed to give visual depth.

FIREPLACE ARRANGEMENT
· · ·

A fireplace is the focal point of a room, but without a fire, an empty grate can be an eyesore. Turn this to your advantage by filling the hearth with an arrangement of flowers.

In the absence of real flames, this display substitutes the bright, fiery reds, oranges and yellows of scarlet plume, alstroemeria, tulips, lilies and chrysanthemums. This colour palette is given depth and richness by the purple of eustoma. The languid forms of ruscus, with the stark outlines of birch twigs, define the architecture of the arrangement.

1 Soak the plastic foam in water and secure in the basket using florist's adhesive tape. Place the basket in the grate of the fireplace.

2 Arrange the ruscus and the birch twigs to create a foliage outline, taking advantage of the natural curves of the ruscus to achieve a flowing effect.

3 Use the scarlet plume to reinforce the outline and define the height of the display. The lilies are the focal flowers and should be arranged to follow roughly a diagonal through the display. The alstroemeria should be positioned to follow the opposite diagonal. Decrease the length of the stems of both flowers from the rear to the front.

4 Arrange the spray chrysanthemums, approximately following, and thus reinforcing, the line of lilies. Again reduce the chrysanthemum stem height from rear to front. Finally, distribute the tulips and eustoma evenly through the arrangement using the most open of the eustoma blooms towards the centre.

ARUM LILY VASE

· · ·

Pure in colour and form, elegant and stately, the arum lily has the presence to be displayed on its own, supported by the minimum of well-chosen foliage. Here it is arranged with the wonderfully curious contorted willow and the large, simple leaves of aucuba. Because they do not compete visually, the willow and the aucuba serve purely as a backdrop to the beauty of the arum.

MATERIALS

· · ·

vase

· · ·

scissors

· · ·

branches of contorted willow

· · ·

6 arum lilies

· · ·

2 bushy branches aucuba 'Gold Dust'

1 Fill the vase to approximately three-quarters with water. Arrange the contorted willow in the vase to establish the overall height of the arrangement. (When cutting a willow stem to the right length, cut the base at a 45° angle and scrape the bark off to approximately 5 cm (2 in) from the end, then split this section.)

The choice of container is of great importance, the visual requirement being for simple unfussy shapes, with glass and metal being particularly appropriate. The chosen vase should complement the sculptural impact of the arum.

2 Arrange the arum lilies at different heights throughout the willow to achieve a visual balance. The willow stems will help support the blooms.

3 Give visual substance to the display by adding stems of aucuba throughout to provide a dark backdrop to throw the arum blooms into sharp relief.

CANDELABRA TABLE
DECORATION
· · ·

Never leave burning candles
unattended and do not allow
them to burn down to within
less than 5 cm (2 in) of the
display height.

The classic combination of flowers and candlelight is usually associated with romantic dinners for two. However, this candelabra table decoration is appropriate to a variety of special dining occasions. Stately candles floating on a sumptuous sea of white lilies and purple asters make a decoration suitable for even the most formal of events.

1 Soak the plastic foam ring in cold water and position the candelabra within the ring. As the arrangement will eventually involve ivy being attached to both the candelabra and ring, it is advisable to create this display *in situ*. Using approximately 10 cm (4 in) long stems of viburnum and variegated pieris, push into the foam to create an even foliage outline.

2 Cut the lily heads leaving about 7.5 cm (3 in) of stem to push into the foam. Group the heads in threes around the circumference of the foam ring. Generally the groups should have one open bloom placed towards the centre with two buds at the outside edge of the ring. But in so doing, remember buds will open in 24 hours to fill the areas.

3 Aster flowers usually have a sturdy main stem and several side stems with flowerheads which should be separated. Cut all the aster stems to approximately 10 cm (4 in) lengths, and distribute evenly through the arrangement, pushing firmly into the plastic foam.

4 Ivy will survive out of water for a time but to ensure it remains in good condition for the life of the decoration, push the cut end of the trail (sprig) into the soaked plastic foam before entwining it around the candelabra. For safety reasons, do not allow any ivy leaves to come up over the candleholder's wax guards.

ORANGE ARRANGEMENT
· · ·

MATERIALS
· · ·
wire basket
· · ·
reindeer moss
· · ·
cellophane (plastic wrap)
· · ·
1 block plastic foam
· · ·
knife
· · ·
florist's adhesive tape
· · ·
scissors
· · ·
10 stems salal tips
· · ·
7 stems orange lily
· · ·
10 stems orange tulip
· · ·
20 stems marigold

The matt green of salal tips creates the perfect background for the spectacular zesty orange colour of the three different flowers used in this display. The arrangement is a dome of flowers supported in plastic foam in a wire basket.

1 Line the basket with a layer of reindeer moss, about 3 cm (1½ in) thick, and line the moss with cellophane (plastic wrap). Cut a block of water-soaked plastic foam to fit the basket and tape securely in place.

2 Push the salal tips into the plastic foam to create a dome-shaped foliage outline in proportion with the container. Salal tips have relatively large rounded leaves which generally should be used sparingly to avoid overwhelming the flowers. However, the strength of the colour and shape of the flowers in this particular arrangement works well with the bold salal leaves.

3 Cut the lily stems to a length to suit the foliage framework and push into the foam evenly throughout the arrangement to reinforce the overall shape.

4 Distribute the tulips evenly through the display, remembering they will continue to grow and their natural downward curve will tend to straighten.

5 Add the marigolds last, positioning them evenly throughout the display. Remember the marigold stems are soft, so take care when pushing them into the plastic foam.

There are two points worth remembering. First the tulips will continue to grow and straighten in the plastic foam, so make allowance for this in your dome shape; second, any buds on the lilies will open, so give them the space to do so.

DECORATED VASE WITH CALLA LILIES

· · ·

MATERIALS

· · ·

a selection of lichen-covered twigs

· · ·

glass vase

· · ·

raffia

· · ·

scissors

· · ·

10 red antirrhinums

· · ·

15 calla lilies

· · ·

3 calla lily leaves

By making the twigs project above the top of the vase, they become an integral part of the arrangement and provide helpful support for the flowers. An alternative look could be created by gluing the heads of dried flowers, such as sunflowers, all over a plain glass vase.

A novel and simple way to transform a container is to decorate its outside with organic material. This example uses lichen-covered twigs and is particularly practical since after the arrangement in the vase has died the twigs will have dried out and, with careful handling, can be kept on the vase for the next display.

1 The twigs have to be fixed securely to the vase. To do this, make two lengths of bundles of raffia and lay on these sufficient twigs to go around the circumference of the vase. Place the vase on its side, on the twigs, and tie firmly with the lengths of raffia. Trim the twig stems level with the base of the vase.

2 Stand the vase upright and three-quarter fill with water. Begin with the red antirrhinums, placing them towards the back to establish the height and width of the arrangement's framework.

3 Distribute the calla lily blooms evenly throughout the arrangement, varying their heights to achieve a visual balance and a good profile. Add the calla lily leaves diagonally through the arrangement, reducing their height from the back to the front. This will visually emphasize the depth of the arrangement.

WINTER TWIGS
ARRANGEMENT
. . .

Cut flowers can be expensive during the winter months but this does not mean flower arranging has to stop. This display is created from the types of winter growth found in domestic gardens. It is simple to arrange and offers a scale suitable to decorate a large space.

Delicate lichen softens the otherwise rough branches of larch while the beautiful and scented winter-flowering viburnum adds a touch of spring. Finally the deep red stems of red-barked dogwood provide a strength of colour which will persist throughout the life of the display and even beyond if dried.

MATERIALS
. . .
5 stems lichen-covered larch twigs
. . .
scissors and secateurs
. . .
large ceramic pot
. . .
5-10 stems red-barked dogwood (Cornus alba)
. . .
10 stems Viburnum x bodnantense 'Dawn'

1 Cut the larch twigs so that the majority are at the maximum height of the display, and arrange to the outline shape. The container should be about one-third of the overall display height.

2 Cut the red-barked dogwood and arrange amongst the larch twigs so that the stems at the rear of the display are at their maximum height, becoming shorter towards the front.

As a general rule when using twigs, remember to strip the stem ends of bark and lichen otherwise they will rot, accelerate the formation of bacteria, shorten the life of the display and very quickly cause the water to smell.

3 Add the flowering viburnum, again varying its length from tall at the rear to shorter at the front. To avoid rotting, be sure to strip off all bark and flowers from the stem ends in the water and split any thick woody stems to allow water in.

HERB OBELISK

· · ·

MATERIALS

· · ·

ruler

· · ·

pencil

· · ·

1 block plastic foam

· · ·

sharp knife

· · ·

suitable container

· · ·

7 radishes

· · ·

8 button mushrooms

· · ·

9 small, clean new potatoes

· · ·

.71 wires

· · ·

scissors

· · ·

dill

· · ·

curry plant

· · ·

marjoram

· · ·

mint

· · ·

bay leaves

The urn container gives the obelisk a grand look, but a less formal, more rustic feel can be achieved by using a terracotta plant pot or mossy basket.

A colourful pillar of herbs and vegetables which looks wonderful on its own and even more striking when used in pairs. It is particularly suitable for a buffet table decoration but can also be used simply as a decorative object in any appropriate setting.

1 Using a ruler and pencil score the cutting lines on the block of plastic foam. Carve the block to the required shape using a sharp knife. Soak the carved plastic foam shape and secure firmly in your chosen container.

2 Wire all the vegetables by pushing a .71 wire through from one side to the other, leaving sufficient wire projecting on both sides to allow you to pull down and out of the base to approximately 4 cm (1½ in). Mushrooms are very fragile and particular care must be taken when wiring these. Having decided on the order you want to use the vegetables, work from the bottom of the obelisk upwards, pushing the wires into the plastic foam to position the vegetables in horizontal rings around the shape.

3 Fill in the gaps between rings of vegetables, using a different herb for each ring. Finally select a quantity of bay leaves of similar size and insert them into the plastic foam under the bottom layer of vegetables to create a formal border.

Right: Detail of the final arrangement

PARROT TULIP CANDLE
DECORATION
· · ·

*plastic foam ring, 15 cm (6 in)
diameter, and holder*

· · ·

*candle, 7.5 x 22.5 cm
(3 x 9 in)*

· · ·

scissors

· · ·

*approximately 7-8 very open
'Parrot' tulip heads*

*Other flowers, such as roses
and buttercups can, when their
flowerheads are full, have their
useful lives extended by the use
of this technique.
Never leave a burning candle
unattended and do not allow it
to burn down to within less
than 5 cm (2 in) of the
display height.*

T here is a tendency to think that a fully opened bloom is at the end of its useful life. However, these Parrot tulip heads have had their lives extended by the
simple process of shortening their stems. The red and yellow of the spreading
petals of these tulips create an impression of flames licking up the candle.

1 Soak the plastic foam
ring in water and
position the candle at its
centre. Check that the
candle is firmly in position.

2 Cut the tulips to a stem
length of approximately
3 cm (1¼ in) and push
them into the plastic foam.
Repeat this around the
entire ring making sure no
foam is left exposed.

BERRIED CANDLE
DECORATION
• • •

A commercially-produced red candle in an earthenware pot can be made into a sumptuous table decoration by embellishing it with fruits and foliage from the garden and hedge. This is a technically simple, yet effective, decoration involving sitting the pot in a small wire basket through which the stems of fruit and foliage are artfully woven.

MATERIALS
. . .
candle in an earthenware pot
. . .
small square wire basket, to
accommodate the pot
. . .
Virginia creeper leaves
on stems
. . .
blackberry clusters on stems
. . .
scissors
. . .
rosehip clusters on stems
. . .
.32 silver reel (rose) wire

1 Place the candle pot in the wire basket. Weave Virginia creeper stems through the wire basket around its entire top edge. Then establish a thick garland of Virginia creeper leaves around the basket.

2 For safe handling strip the thorns from the blackberry stems and cut to approximately 6 cm (2 in) long. Push the stems into the Virginia creeper garland and through the wire basket.

The plant materials used are robust enough to survive in good condition for a day or two out of water but would benefit from mist spraying. Never leave burning candles unattended and do not allow them to burn down to within 5 cm (2 in) of the display.

3 Using the same procedure, add the rosehips but in separate small groups around the circumference of the basket. If the decoration is likely to be moved, it is safer to provide additional security for the stems by tying them to the basket with lengths of fine silver reel (rose) wire.

SECTION TWO

• • •

NEW WAYS WITH DRIED FLOWERS

• • •

Capture the very essence of nature with these imaginative dried flower arrangements. From sweet-smelling posies of roses and lavender to spectacular floral wreaths and garlands, the following pages will show you how to create beautiful displays that will last for many months. Introducing a wide range of dried flowers, grasses and foliage as well as sea shells and starfish, the displays are lively and contemporary in feel and will challenge both beginner and expert alike.

INTRODUCTION
. . .

*Right: Dried Flower Tussie
Mussies (page 166)*

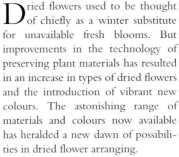

Dried flowers used to be thought of chiefly as a winter substitute for unavailable fresh blooms. But improvements in the technology of preserving plant materials has resulted in an increase in types of dried flowers and the introduction of vibrant new colours. The astonishing range of materials and colours now available has heralded a new dawn of possibilities in dried flower arranging.

*Above: Decorated Pot Display
(page 110)*

*Right: Crescent Moon Wreath
(page 176)*

Today's approach to dried flower displays is to emphasize colour and texture by using massed materials so that the collective strength of their qualities creates the impact. Even where a number of varieties are incorporated in a display they should be used in clusters to extract the maximum effect. It is wise to avoid using individual stems of a particular material because this will make for rather bitty looking displays.

To get the best out of dried plant material, do not be afraid to integrate other materials with them: dried fruits, gourds, seashells, roots and driftwood can all add an extra dimension to a display. To create an opulent effect, bunches of dried herbs and spices and varieties of dried and preserved mosses can be added and groups of filled terracotta pots may be attached. With all this choice today's dried

Above: Apple and Lavender Topiary Tree (page 112)

Left: Peony and Apple Table Arrangement (page 118)

flower display is a far cry from the fading brown and orange dust traps of the past.

Impressive though improvements in preserving plant materials may be, the ravages of time, sunlight, moisture and dust still take their toll on dried flowers. Do not make the mistake of believing dried arrangements will last for ever. A useful life of around six months is the best that can be expected before dried flowers begin to look dusty and faded.

However, by taking a few simple common sense precautions, the life of a dried arrangement can be maximized. To avoid fading, keep the arrangement out of direct sunlight. Do not allow dried flowers to become damp and particularly be aware of condensation in bathrooms and on window ledges. To prevent the build-up of dust give the arrangement an occasional blast with a hair-dryer set on slow and cool. When the arrangement is new, spray it with hair lacquer to help prevent the dropping of grass seeds and petals, but do not use hair-spray on dust-covered dried flowers.

Below: Rose and Starfish Wreath (page 120)

A potentially rewarding aspect of dried flower arranging is drying and preserving the plant material yourself. It takes patience and organization but with application you will be able to preserve materials not commercially available and, since some dried flowers can be expensive, you will save yourself money.

There are different methods of preservation to suit different plant materials. In the following pages, these methods are clearly explained. There is also a list of materials with the appropriate drying method for each. The list is not exhaustive so if the material you want to preserve is not referred to, then assess its characteristics, find a similar type and try the method recommended for that.

DRYING TECHNIQUES
· · ·

AIR DRYING
Probably the simplest method of preserving plant material is to air dry it. Air drying is the generic term for a number of techniques but fundamentally it is the preservation of plant materials without the use of chemicals or desiccants.

The ideal environment for air drying will be dark, warm, clean, dust-free, well ventilated and, most importantly, dry. Typically, attics, boiler rooms or large airing cupboards are the locations where these conditions are found.

HARVESTING MATERIALS
If you are preserving material you have grown yourself, be sure it is as dry as possible when you harvest it. Choose a dry day after the morning dew has disappeared and before the damp of evening begins to settle.

It is also important to harvest materials at the right point in their development, to ensure colours remain vibrant and petals do not drop. Experience will teach you about any variations from plant to plant, but in general the time to harvest is when the material is neither too young nor too mature – when the flowers have developed from bud to open bloom but are still young, fresh and firm. Seed pods and grasses must be just

Selecting the right drying method for a plant comes with experience.

fully developed – any more and the seeds may drop.

If you buy commercially grown materials to dry yourself, bear in mind the general principles of harvesting when you select them, and remember, drying must take place as soon as possible after harvesting or purchasing the plant materials.

AIR DRYING BY HANGING PLANT MATERIAL
In most instances the foliage on flowers does not dry as well as the blooms so, when your materials are fresh, remove the leaves from the lower half of the stems before drying.

As a rule plant materials are bunched together in groups of not more than 10 stems and each bunch should contain only one plant variety. Stems should be all around the same length with all their heads at the same level. Do not pack the heads too tightly together as this will inhibit the circulation of air around them and may distort their final dried shape.

Secure the stem ends together with twine, raffia or a rubber band. The stems will shrink as they dry so a rubber band is probably most practical because it will contract with them to maintain a firm hold.

Hang the bunches in a suitable environment in a safe position, high enough so that they will not be disturbed and with their heads down and stems vertical.

Drying rates vary from plant to plant and are subject to factors such as atmospheric conditions, bunch sizes and temperatures but it is essential that you make sure the materials are thoroughly dried before using them. This will be when the thickest part of the flowerhead has dried and when bending the stem causes it to snap. Any moisture retained in plant

The weight of the flowerheads help keep the stems straight.

materials will cause mould, resulting in drooping and shrivelling.

It should be noted that some materials which can be dried with this method should not be hung with their heads down. In particular physalis, with its pendulous orange Chinese lanterns, would look unnatural if dried upside-down. Instead, hook individual physalis stems over a horizontal length of twine in their upright growing attitude.

AIR DRYING PLANT MATERIAL ON A RACK
Some plants such as *Daucus cariba* (Queen Anne's lace) can be air dried, but their florets will curl up if they are hung upside-down.

Instead, make a rack from a piece of small mesh wire, place it in a suitable environment, and drop the stem down through the mesh so that it is held by its bloom. With the flower facing upwards, it will dry well.

Hydrangea heads and gypsophila can both be air dried with their stems in water.

AIR DRYING PLANT MATERIALS WITH THEIR STEM ENDS IN WATER

This is the method of preservation for those types of flowers which have a tendency to wilt before the drying process is completed. It is sometimes called the "evaporation technique" and is particularly suitable for hydrangea, allium and heather.

Cut the bottoms of stems at an angle of 45 degrees and place them in a container with a depth of about 7.5 cm (3 in) of water and place the container in a suitable environment. This slows down the drying process to give the plant material time to dry fully in a natural position and without deterioration in the condition of the blooms.

AIR DRYING IN A "NATURAL" ATTITUDE

Some materials benefit from being dried in an upright position so that they retain a more natural shape.

Simply stand the material in the sort of container in which you might make an arrangement, place it in a suitable environment and it will dry in its natural shape. Grasses and stems of mimosa are suitable for this method.

However, with some material this method can produce extraordinary results. The normally straight stems of bear grass *(Xerophyllum tenax)* will, when placed in a short container, form themselves into attractive ringlets as they dry. A simple alternative method for drying grasses is to lie them flat on paper in a suitable environment and they will retain a satisfactory shape.

DESICCANT DRYING

A particularly effective method of preservation is drying by the use of a desiccant such as sand, borax or, best of all, silica gel. The desiccant absorbs all the moisture from the plant material. This can be a time-consuming process but it is well worth the effort because the result is dried materials, with colour and form nearer their fresh condition than can be achieved by almost any other method of preservation.

This method is essential for the preservation of fleshy flowerheads that cannot be successfully air dried. Flowers such as lilies, tulips, freesias, pansies and open garden roses all respond well to desiccant drying and provide the flower arranger with a wealth of preserved materials not generally commercially available.

For the flower arranger there is little point in using this method for flower materials that air dry well because on a non-commercial scale desiccant drying is only suitable for small amounts of material and silica gel is expensive.

Flowers to be preserved by this method must be in perfect, healthy condition and harvested preferably after a few hours in the sun, with as little surface moisture as possible.

It is important to choose a drying method which will allow the plant material to retain its original colour and form.

There are flowers and materials from every season suitable for drying.

WIRING FLOWERS FOR DESICCANT DRYING

Desiccant drying is normally only used for flowerheads as the process weakens stems to the extent that they become virtually unusable. Also, it should be remembered that the flowerheads themselves will become very fragile. Indeed, if you are going to make wire stems it should be done while the flowers are still fresh before beginning the desiccant process.

Flowers with hollow stems, like zinnias, are wired by inserting the wire through their natural stem and pushing it into the flowerhead. Be careful not to push it too far because the flowerhead will shrink as it dries and this might expose an unsightly wire. Heavy petalled flowers like dahlias have to be dried face up, so only provide them with short wired stems. These stems can be extended after the flowers have been dried. Flowers which have woody, tough or very thin stems may be wired through the seed box (calyx) at the base of the flowerhead from one side to the other. Bring the projecting wire ends down and form them into a mount.

During the drying process the flower and stem will shrink so a double or single leg mount will become loose and slide off unless its wire has been securely pushed into the stem while the flower was still fresh. Remember that you still need to make the gauge of wire used for a mount compatible with the weight of the flower when it is fresh.

DRYING WITH SILICA GEL

Nowadays silica gel is considered a superior material to borax or sand for desiccant drying. Sand and borax are heavy and great care must be taken to avoid damaging flowers dried in these materials. Silica gel on the other hand is lightweight and can be crushed very fine so it can be worked into complicated petal configurations without causing damage.

Flowers dry very quickly in silica gel, five to ten days being the usual time necessary for most plant material. Borax and sand are much slower and it can take up to five weeks to dry some materials! Use an airtight container when using silica gel as it absorbs moisture from the air, whereas sand and borax can be used in any container provided it has a lid. The method for sand and borax is generally the same as for silica gel.

Some silica gel crystals are blue and this changes to pink as they absorb moisture which will help you measure the progress of the drying process.

1 When you have prepared your silica gel crystals place a layer approximately 5 cm (2 in) deep in the bottom of your container. Place the flowerheads in the crystals face down or if the petals are complex face up. If their stems are wire mounted, bend them as necessary to fit the flowers into the container.

2 When all flowerheads are in position, spoon a second 5 cm (2 in) deep layer of silica gel over them to cover completely. Be sure to fill all parts of the flowerhead with crystals. If it has complex petals, lift them carefully with a toothpick and gently push the crystals into every crevice. Put the lid on the container and tape around to make airtight.

Since each flower type will probably require a different time to dry, check progress at regular intervals. Flowers left too long in a desiccant will eventually disintegrate. When you start using this method, there will, of course, be an element of trial and error before you are able to establish the time necessary for each flower type.

Some flowers with a deep cupped shape, such as tulips, should be dried individually in a plastic cup of crystals sealed with clear film to ensure they keep their shape.

After you remove the dried flowers from the silica gel, they will probably still have powder on them and this must be removed very carefully with a fine, soft paintbrush.

You can, of course, re-use the silica gel over and over again. All you need to do is spread it out on a tray and leave it in a warm oven until it is dry. This will be easy to recognize in the coloured silica because it will become blue again.

MICROWAVE METHOD

The silica gel process can be accelerated by using a microwave oven. Remember, however, that you must not put wired materials in a microwave oven. Any wiring will have to be done after drying which may be difficult given the fragility of the dried blooms.

Bury the material in silica gel in a container, but do not put a lid on it. Instead, place the uncovered container in the microwave oven with about half a cup of water next to it.

Set the microwave timer according to the type of flower you are drying. Delicate blooms may take less than two minutes while more fleshy flowers will take longer. You will need to experiment with your timing to get accurate settings. After the process is ended leave the silica to cool before removing the flowers.

STORAGE OF DESICCANT DRIED MATERIALS

To keep desiccant dried materials in good condition store them in an airtight container, packed loosely with layers of tissue paper inbetween.

Place a small pouch of silica gel in the container to absorb any moisture, taking care not to get the silica in direct contact with the flowers.

Of course, there are plenty of materials dried by Nature to try in a display.

PRESERVING WITH GLYCERINE

Foliage in particular does not respond well to air drying. Its green colours fade and the result is tired-looking, brittle material. Happily the use of glycerine works well for many varieties of foliage.

This method enables plant material to replace the moisture which has evaporated from its stems and leaves by absorption of a solution of glycerine and water.

Because this process relies on the ability of plant material to draw up the solution it is not suitable for autumn foliage which has, of course, already died. Indeed, it is important that materials to be treated with glycerine are harvested in the middle of their growing season, when the leaves are young but developed and are full of moisture. Foliage that is too young and is soft and pale green does not respond to glycerine.

The stem ends of material to be treated should be cut at an angle of 45 degrees and the lower leaves stripped. Peel the bark off the bottom 6 cm (2½ in) of the stem and split the end up to about 10 cm (4 in) to ensure efficient absorption of the solution.

Mix one part glycerine with two parts hot water and pour the solution into a substantial container to a depth of about 20 cm (8 in). The size of container will depend on the amount of material to be treated. Stand the stems of foliage in the solution for anything from two to six weeks, depending on the size and texture of the leaves, to achieve full absorption. Always keep an eye on the amount of solution in the container and top it up as necessary to maintain the level.

If you are treating individual leaves they can be completely submerged in the solution, but a thicker half-glycerine, half-water mixture should be used. It will take two to three weeks for leaves to be properly treated, after which time remove them from the solution and wipe off any excess.

Glycerine treatment works best for mature, sturdy plant material such as beech, hornbeam, magnolia and elaeagnus. Surprisingly it is also successful with less robust material like *Molucella laevis* (bells of Ireland) and trails of ivy.

As materials are preserved their leaves will change colour to a variety of shades of brown. When all the leaves have changed colour you will know the process is complete. The visual results on materials of treatment with glycerine may vary even for the same material but with increasing experience of the technique you will become better able to predict what you are likely to achieve. Berried foliage can also be preserved with glycerine but the berries will shrink slightly and change colour.

An advantage of glycerine-preserved foliage is that it remains malleable, and dusty leaves can be wiped with a damp cloth.

PLANT PRESERVATION TECHNIQUES

· · ·

The following is a list of plants and materials and the drying method suitable for each. The list is not exhaustive, so if you find a plant you wish to try drying, assess its characteristics, find a similar type and try the drying method for that.

COMMON NAME	LATIN NAME	PLANT SECTION	TECHNIQUE
African marigold	Tagetes	flower	air drying
anemone (windflower)	Anemone	flower	air drying desiccant
asparagus	Asparagus plumosus	leaf	microwave
aspidistra	Aspidistra	leaf	glycerine
astilbe	Astilbe	flower	air drying
bay	Laurus	leaf	desiccant/glycerine
bear's breeches	Acanthus	flower spike / leaf	air drying glycerine
beech	Fagus	leaf	glycerine
bellflower	Campanula	flower	air drying
bell heather	Erica cinerea	flower	air drying
bells of Ireland	Moluccella laevis	bract	air drying/glycerine
blackberry (bramble)	Robus (Rosaceae)	leaf / berry	glycerine
blanket flower	Gaillardia	seedhead	air drying
broom	Cytisus	flower spray	air drying/desiccant
bulrush	Typha latifolia	seedhead	air drying
buttercup	Ranunculus	flower	desiccant
camellia	Camellia	flower	desiccant
campion (catchfly)	Silene	flower	air drying
candytuft	Iberis	flower / seedhead	dessicant / air drying
caraway	Carum carvi	seedhead	air drying
carnation	Dianthus	flower	desiccant
celosia	Celosia	flower	air drying/ air drying in water
chamomile	Chamaemelum nobile Athemis	flower	air drying/ air drying in water
Chinese lantern	Physalis	stems and seedheads	air drying
chive	Allium schoenoprasum	flower	air drying/ air drying in water
choisya	Choisya	leaf	glycerine
chrysanthemum	Chrysanthemum	flower	desiccant
clarkia	Clarkia (syn Godetia)	flower	air drying
clematis (old man's beard, travellers' joy)	Clematis	leaf / seedhead	air drying / air drying

COMMON NAME	LATIN NAME	PLANT SECTION	TECHNIQUE
cock's-foot grass	Dactylis glomerata	stems and seedheads	air drying
copper beech	Fagus sylvatica	leaf	air drying/glycerine
cornflower (bluebottle)	Centaurea cyanus	flower	air drying/ microwave/ air drying in water
corn cob	Zea mays	seedhead	air drying
cotinus	Cotinus	flower / leaf	air drying / glycerine
cow parsley	Anthriscus sylvestris	seedhead	air drying
daffodil	Narcissus	flower	desiccant
dahlia	Dahlia	flower	desiccant
daisy	Bellis	flower	desiccant
delphinium	Delphinium	flower spike	air drying/desiccant
dock	Rumex	seedhead	air drying
dryandra	Dryandra	flower	air drying
elaeagnus	Elaeagnus	leaf	glycerine/ microwave
eucalyptus	Eucalyptus	leaf	air drying/glycerine
fennel	Foeniculum vulgare	leaf / seedhead	air drying microwave / air drying
ferns		leaf	glycerine
fescue grass	Festuca	stems and seedheads	air drying
feverfew	Chrysanthemum parthenium	flower	air drying/ air drying in water/ microwave
fig	Ficus	leaf	glycerine
forsythia	Forsythia	flower sprays	desiccant
foxglove	Digitalis	flower	desiccant
freesia	Freesia	flower	desiccant
gay feathers	Liatris	flower spikes	air drying
geranium (cranesbill)	Geranium	leaf and flower	desiccant
giant hogweed	Heracleum mantegazzianum	stem and seedhead	air drying
globe amaranth	Gomphrena globosa	flowers	air drying
globe thistle	Echinops	thistle heads	air drying
golden rod	Solidago	flower	air drying microwave
grape hyacinth	Muscari	flower	desiccant
gypsophila	Gypsophila	flower	air drying/ air drying in water/ microwave
hare's-tail grass	Lagarus ovatus	stems and seedheads	air drying
heather	Erica	flower spikes	air drying in water/ glycerine
helichrysum	Helichrysum	flower	air drying
holly	Ilex	leaf	glycerine
hollyhock	Alcea	flower	desiccant
honesty	Lunaria	seedhead	air drying
hop	Humulus	leaf and bracts	air drying/glycerine
hosta (plantain lily)	Hosta	leaf	glycerine

COMMON NAME	LATIN NAME	PLANT SECTION	TECHNIQUE
hyacinth	*Hyacinthus*	flower	desiccant
hydrangea	*Hydrangea*	flower and bracts	air drying/ air drying in water/ microwave
ivy	*Hedera*	leaf	glycerine
Japanese aralia	*Fatsia japonica*	leaf	glycerine
Jerusalam sage	*Phlomis fruticosa*	flower, leaf and seedhead	air drying
kerria (Jew's mallow)	*Kerria*	flowers	air drying
knapweed	*Centaurea*	seedhead	air drying
lady's mantle	*Alchemilla mollis*	flower	air drying/ microwave
larkspur	*Consolida*	flower spike	air drying/desiccant
laurel	*Laurus*	leaf	glycerine
lavender	*Lavandula*	flower spikes	air drying/ air drying in water
lavender cotton	*Santolina chamaecyparissus*	leaf	air drying/ microwave
lilac	*Syringa*	small flower sprays	desiccant
lily	*Lilium*	flower	desiccant
lily-of-the-valley	*Convallaria*	flower	desiccant
linseed	*Linum usitatissium*	stems and seedheads	air drying
London pride	*Saxifraga x urbium*	flower	desiccant
Love-in-a-mist	*Nigella damascena*	flower and seedhead	air drying
love-lies-bleeding	*Amaranthus caudatus*	flower spike	air drying
lupin	*Lupinus*	flower seedhead	desiccant air drying
magnolia	*Magnolia*	flower	desiccant
maple	*Acer*	leaf	glycereine
marguerite	*Chrysanthemum frutescens*	flower	desiccant
marjoram	*Origanum*	flower	air drying microwave
Mexican giant hyssop	*Agastache*	flower	air drying
millet	*Panicum miliaceum*	seedhead	air drying
mimosa	*Acacia*	flower sprays	air drying/desiccant air drying in water
mullein	*Verbascum*	seedhead	air drying
narcissus	*Narcissus*	flower	glycerine
oats	*Avena sativa*	stems and seedheads	air drying
onion	*Allium*	flower	air drying in water/ air drying
orchid	*Orchidacea*	flower	desiccant
pampas grass	*Cortaderia selloana*	stems and seedheads	air drying
pansy	*Viola wittrockiana*	flower	desiccant
pearl everlasting	*Anaphalis*	flower	air drying/ air drying in water
peony	*Paeonia*	flower	air drying/desiccant
pine	*Pinus*	cones	air drying
pinks	*Dianthus*	flower	desiccant
polyanthus	*Primula*	flower	desiccant
poppy	*Papaver*	seedhead	air drying
pot marigold	*Calendula officinalis*	flower	air drying/desiccant
phalaris	*Phalaris*	stems and seedheads	air drying

COMMON NAME	LATIN NAME	PLANT SECTION	TECHNIQUE
primrose	*Primula vulgaris*	flower	desiccant
quaking grass	*Briza*	stems and seedheads	air drying upright or hanging
rhododendron	*Rhododendron*	leaf	glycerine microwave
rose	*Rosa*	bud, flower, leaf fully open flower hip	air drying desiccant glycerine
rosemary	*Rosmarinus officinalis*	leaf spike	glycerine/air drying microwave
rue	*Ruta graveolens*	seedhead	air drying
safflower	*Carthamus tinctorius*	flower	air drying
sage	*Salvia officinalis*	flower and leaf	air drying
sea holly	*Eryngium*	flower	air drying
sea lavender	*Limonium*	flower	air drying/ air drying in water
sedge	*Carex*	seedhead	air drying
sedum (stonecrop)	*Sedum*	flower	air drying/desiccant microwave
senecio	*Senecio*	leaf	air drying/ microwave
shoofly	*Nicandra phyusalodes*	seedpods	air drying
sorrel tree	*Oxydendrum arboreum*	seedhead	air drying
statice	*Psylliostachys*	flower	air drying
stock	*Matthiola*	flower	dessicant
strawflower	*Helichrysum bracteatum*	flower	air drying
sunflower	*Helianthus*	flower	air drying
sweet pea	*Lathyrus odoratus*	flower	desiccant
sweet William	*Dianthus barbatus*	flower	air dry quickly
tansy	*Tanacetum vulgare*	flower	air drying/ microwave
teasel	*Dipsacus fullonum*	seedhead	air drying
thistle	*Carlina*	seedhead	air drying
wheat (bearded)	*Triticale*	stems and seedheads	air drying
wheat (common)	*Triticum aestiuum*	stems and seedheads	air drying
tulip	*Tulipa*	flower	desiccant
vine	*Vitus*	leaf	desiccant
wallflower	*Cheiranthus*	flower	desiccant
winged spindle	*Euonymus alatus*	flower	air drying
xeranthemum (immortelle)	*Xeranthemum*	flower	air drying
yarrow	*Achillea millefolium*	flower	air drying
zinnia	*Zinnia*	flower	desiccant

CONTEMPORARY WREATHS
· · ·

MATERIALS
· · ·
RED AND YELLOW
MATERIALS
scissors
· · ·
34 red roses
· · ·
33 yellow roses
· · ·
florist's adhesive
· · ·
plastic foam ring for dried
flowers, 10 cm (4 in) diameter
· · ·
ribbon
· · ·
BLUE AND WHITE
MATERIALS
scissors
· · ·
25 white roses
· · ·
26 small heads blue globe
thistle
· · ·
glue
· · ·
plastic foam ring for dried
flowers, 10 cm (4 in) diameter
· · ·
ribbon

*The wreaths are simple to
make but will require a lot of
material and a little patience to
achieve the neat checker-board
patterns that characterize them.*

These two wall-hanging decorations show how massed dried flowers in strong contrasting colours can create a striking contemporary display.

One display couples white roses with blue globe thistles, the second red roses with yellow roses; but alternative materials can be used provided all the flower-heads used in any display are about the same size as each other. Consider using green *Nigella orientalis* with white roses, bleached white poppy seed heads with bright yellow helichrysums or blue sea holly with bright orange carthamus.

1 For the red and yellow wreath, cut the rose stems to 2.5 cm (1 in). Around the outside edge of the foam ring, form a circle of alternating yellow and red roses by gluing on their stems and pushing them into the foam. Leave a small gap in the rose circle for a ribbon. Inside the first circle, construct a second circle, offsetting the colours against the first ring.

2 Continue building circles of roses until the ring is covered. Pass the ribbon through the centre and around the gap on the plastic foam ring. Use the ribbon to hang the wreath or tie in a bow. Follow the same method for the second wreath.

TERRACOTTA PLANT-POT DISPLAY

· · ·

This delightful selection of dried flower arrangements in terracotta pots shows the exciting colours and types of flowers now available. Massed flowers in bright colours are presented in a contemporary way but in old-fashioned terracotta thumb (rose) pots, the rustic charm of which has been enhanced by colouring their surfaces.

The display will have the greatest impact when used as a group but you could place them individually around the rooms of your house if you prefer.

MATERIALS

· · ·

1 block plastic foam for dried
flowers

· · ·

knife

· · ·

5 old-fashioned terracotta pots,
coloured with chalk

· · ·

scissors

· · ·

16 pink dried roses

· · ·

7 dried sunflower heads

· · ·

1 bunch dried lavender

· · ·

25 small cinnamon sticks

· · ·

10 stems Craspedia globosa

· · ·

9 stems blue globe thistle

1 Cut the plastic foam for each pot and wedge it in so that it is about 2 cm (¾ in) below the rim. Cut all the stems so that when they are pushed into the plastic foam only their heads are visible above the rim of the pot. Fill one pot with tightly massed rose heads. In the second pot, push the sunflower heads into the plastic foam. Again, make sure that only the heads are visible above the rim of the pot. The aim is to achieve a massed domed effect in each pot.

Even the least experienced flower arranger will have no difficulty in creating these charming arrangements

2 Fill the third pot with lavender stems, cut so that the bottoms of the flower spikes are level with the rim of the pot. Break the cinnamon sticks to create jagged ends, making them about 10 cm (4 in) long. Push them into the foam of the fourth pot, with the tops slightly varying in height. Cut the *Craspedia* and the globe thistle stems so their heads will appear just above the rim of the pot. Fill the fifth pot by creating a regular pattern of blue globe thistle in a yellow carpet of *Craspedia*.

109

DECORATED POT DISPLAY
. . .

MATERIALS
. . .
knife
. . .
*1 block plastic foam for dried
flowers*
. . .
*hand-painted terracotta plant
pot*
. . .
florist's adhesive tape
. . .
.71 wires
. . .
reindeer moss
. . .
scissors
. . .
20 stems small globe thistles
. . .
20 bleached cane spirals
. . .
30 stems dried white roses

*The display is basically
massed dried flowers with the
addition of curly cane spirals to
add height and humour. It is
quick-and-easy to make and
would be a fun decoration for a
child's bedroom.*

This display is purely for fun. The container is a terracotta pot decorated with a painted head against a bright blue background. You can decorate a terra-cotta pot with your own design and create a complementary floral display for it.

As a general rule, if the container is in any way elaborate, then the floral display in it should be simple, but this display is deliberately flamboyant because it is designed to represent hair growing out of the painted head.

1 Cut the block of plastic foam so that it wedges into the decorated pot and extends approximately 4 cm (1¾ in) above the rim. Secure it in place with adhesive tape. Make hairpin shapes from the .71 wire. Tuck reindeer moss between the sides of the pot and the plastic foam and push the wire hairpins through the moss and into the foam to secure.

2 Cut the globe thistle stems to approximately 10 cm (4 in) in length and arrange them throughout the plastic foam to create an even domed shape.

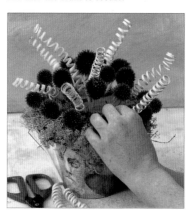

3 Cut the cane spirals to a length of about 15 cm (6 in) and push their stems into the plastic foam, distributing them evenly throughout the globe thistles.

4 Cut the stems of the dried roses to approximately 10 cm (4 in) in length and arrange them evenly amongst the other materials in the display.

APPLE AND LAVENDER TOPIARY TREE

· · ·

MATERIALS

· · ·

terracotta pot, 15 cm (6 in)
diameter

· · ·

cellophane (plastic wrap)

· · ·

sand

· · ·

knife

· · ·

1 block plastic foam for dried
flowers

· · ·

glue

· · ·

1 piece preserved (dried) root
with two branches

· · ·

2 plastic foam balls, 12 cm
(4¾ in) diameter

· · ·

60 slices preserved (dried) apple

· · ·

.71 wires

· · ·

150 stems natural phalaris

· · ·

scissors

· · ·

30 stems cream dried roses

· · ·

50 stems Nigella orientalis

· · ·

20 stems natural ti tree

· · ·

150 stems dried lavender

· · ·

12 short stems preserved
(dried) eucalyptus

Decorative trees are often referred to as topiary trees, and whether made from fresh or dried materials can be designed to match the colour scheme and image of any room.

This dried flower and fruit example has soft soothing colours: pale green phalaris and *Nigella orientalis,* dusty blue lavender, white ti tree, soft grey eucalyptus and the creamy tones of the dried roses and apple slices.

Topiary trees have a tendency to be top heavy, especially if they have more than one branch. To counterbalance this, make sure that the container is weighted with wet sand or, as a more permanent measure, plaster of Paris.

1 Line the terracotta pot with cellophane (plastic wrap) or polythene (plastic sheeting) and three-quarters fill it with wet sand. Cut the block of plastic foam to fit the pot, firmly wedge it in on top of the sand and level it with the rim of the pot.

2 Put a few drops of glue on the base of the piece of root. With its branches pointed upwards, push the root into the centre of the plastic foam in the terracotta pot. Apply a few drops of glue on to the top of the branches and push one of the plastic foam balls on to each branch.

3 Form the apple slices into 20 groups of three. Push a .71 wire through the flesh of a group and bring the ends down, twisting together to form a double leg mount. Cut the phalaris stems to a length of about 3 cm (1¼ in) and form 30 groups of five, double leg mounting each group with .71 wire.

4 Cut the wires of the phalaris groups to approximately 4 cm (1½ in) and distribute them evenly all over the two balls by pushing the wired stems into the plastic foam. Cut the roses to a stem length of approximately 5 cm (2 in) and push the stems into the foam, distributing them evenly among the phalaris.

5 Cut the wire stems of the groups of apple slices to a length of approximately 4 cm (1½ in) and push them in to the foam, distributing them evenly around both balls. Cut 40 stems of the *Nigella orientalis* and all the stems of ti tree to a length of approximately 5 cm (2 in). Push the stems into the foam, distributing both evenly over the two balls.

6 Cut the lavender to an overall length of approximately 5 cm (2 in), form them in to 40 groups of three and push the stems of these groups into the foam. Position them evenly among the other materials on both balls.

7 Cut the eucalyptus stems and the remaining *Nigella orientalis* and lavender stems to varying lengths. At the base of the tree push these stems into the plastic foam to create an arrangement that covers the foam completely.

This tree is relatively intricate to make as it involves wiring and a large quantity of different materials. However, a more unusual effect can be achieved by the use of only one or two materials, for example the roses and the apple slices.

113

OLIVE-OIL CAN ROSE ARRANGEMENT

· · ·

MATERIALS

· · ·

*1 block plastic foam for dried
flowers*

· · ·

knife

· · ·

small rectangular olive oil can

· · ·

scissors

· · ·

*40 stems dried 'Jacaranda'
roses*

· · ·

raffia

*If you come across an eye-
catching container, however
unlikely, remember it may be
just right for a floral display.
And if you are using dried
flowers it does not even need to
be watertight.*

An old olive oil can may not be the first thing to spring to mind when considering a container for your dried flower arrangement, but the bright reds, yellows and greens of this tin make it an attractive option.

Since this container is so striking, the arrangement is kept simple with only one type of flower and one colour used. This creates an effective contemporary display.

1 Cut the plastic foam to fit snugly in the olive oil can, filling it to 2 cm (¾ in) down from its rim.

2 Cut the dried roses so that they protrude about 10 cm (4 in) above the rim of the tin. Starting at the left-hand side of the tin, arrange a line of five tightly packed roses in the plastic foam from its front to its back. Continue arranging lines of five roses parallel to the first and closely packed to each other across the width of the tin.

3 Continue adding lines of roses until the roses are used up. Then take a small bundle of raffia about 3 cm (1¼ in) thick and twist it to make it compact. Loosely wrap the raffia round the stems of the roses just above the top of the tin and finish in a tied knot.

TIED PINK PEONY BOUQUET
. . .

This lovely bouquet demonstrates how, by the use of modern preserving techniques, the strong natural colours of flowers can be retained after drying.

The spiralled bouquet is a loose, slightly domed arrangement that uses its flowers on long stems. The colours are extraordinarily rich for dried flowers, with deep pink roses and peonies and purple marjoram.

1 Lay all the materials in separate groups for easy access when working. Split the marjoram into 15 small bunches. Start building the bouquet by holding a dried peony in your hand about two-thirds the way down its stem. Add two stems of roses, then a small bunch of marjoram and another single peony, turning the bunch in your hand with every addition to make the stems form a spiral. Continue adding materials in this sequence, always turning the bunch in your hand to produce a spiral of stems. Occasionally vary your hand position to create a slightly domed shape.

As a gift, the bouquet would be a beautiful alternative to fresh flowers and since it is already arranged it can be put straight into a container.

2 When all the materials have been incorporated in the bunch, tie twine tightly around the binding point – the point where all the stems cross. Trim the stem ends so they are even and, below the binding point, make up about one-third of the overall height of the bouquet. Finally, tie a ribbon around the binding point and finish in a decorative bow.

SPICY STAR WALL
DECORATION
. . .

*15 cinnamon sticks, 30 cm
(12 in) long*

. . .

raffia

. . .

scissors

. . .

75 lavender stems

. . .

ribbon

*If a Christmas look is
required, substitute dried fruit
slices and gilded seed heads for
the lavender. Similarly, any
sturdy straight twigs can be
used instead of cinnamon.*

This star-shaped wall decoration is constructed from groups of long cinnamon sticks. It is embellished with bunches of lavender to add colour, texture, contrast and a scent which mixes with the warm, spicy smell of the cinnamon.

Its construction requires a bit of patience but is a simple matter of binding the materials together. Take care when handling the cinnamon as it can be brittle.

1 Separate the cinnamon sticks into five groups of three. Interlace the ends of two groups of sticks to form a point and secure firmly by tying them together with raffia. Trim the ends of the raffia.

2 Continue interlacing and binding together groups of cinnamon sticks to create a star-shaped framework. Also, bind together the sticks where they cross each other to make the frame rigid.

3 Separate the lavender into bunches of 15 stems each. Turn the star shape so that the binding knots are at the back and attach the bunches of lavender to the front of the frame, using raffia at the cross points of the cinnamon sticks.

4 When all the lavender bunches have been secured, make a small bow from the ribbon and tie it to the decoration at the bottom crossing point of the cinnamon sticks.

PEONY AND APPLE
TABLE ARRANGEMENT
· · ·

*1 block plastic foam for dried
flowers*

· · ·

knife

· · ·

terracotta bowl

· · ·

florist's adhesive tape

· · ·

scissors

· · ·

*10 stems preserved (dried)
eucalyptus*

· · ·

*18 slices preserved (dried)
apple*

· · ·

.71 wires

· · ·

2 large heads dried hydrangea

· · ·

10 pale pink dried peonies

· · ·

20 deep pink dried roses

· · ·

20 dried peony leaves

· · ·

10 stems ti tree

This delicate arrangement can be made for a specific occasion and kept to be used again and again, whenever a special decoration is called for.

The construction of the decoration is relatively simple, involving the minimum of wiring.

1 Cut the block of plastic foam so that it wedges into the bowl and hold it securely in place with the florist's adhesive tape. Cut the eucalyptus stems to about 13 cm (5 in), making sure that the cut ends are clean of leaves, and arrange them evenly around the plastic foam to create a domed foliage outline to the display.

2 Group the slices of preserved (dried) apple into threes and double leg mount them with .71 wires. Push the six groups of wired apple slices into the foam, distributing them evenly throughout the display. The apple slices should be a little shorter than the eucalyptus when in place.

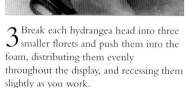

3 Break each hydrangea head into three smaller florets and push them into the foam, distributing them evenly throughout the display, and recessing them slightly as you work.

4 Cut the stems of the peonies to approximately 12 cm (4¾ in) in length and arrange them evenly throughout the display. This time, the peonies should not be recessed.

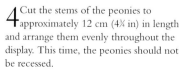

This pretty arrangement is suitable for a small table.

5 Cut the dried rose stems to approximately 13 cm (4¾ in) in length and push them into the plastic foam throughout the other materials in the arrangement.

6 Arrange the dried peony leaves evenly amongst the flowers. Cut the ti tree into stems of approximately 13 cm (4¾ in) in length and distribute them throughout the display.

119

ROSE AND STARFISH WREATH
. . .

MATERIALS
. . .
10 small dried starfish
. . .
.71 wires
. . .
scissors
. . .
florist's adhesive
. . .
*plastic foam ring for dried
flowers, 13 cm (5 in) diameter*
. . .
45 shell-pink dried rose heads
. . .
velvet ribbon

*The construction of this
wreath involves a small
amount of wiring, but is
otherwise straightforward.*

The design of this visually simple wall decoration involves massing a single type of flower and framing them with a halo of geometric shapes, in this case stars. The prettiness of its soft peach colours makes it suitable for a bedroom wall, in which case sprinkle it with scented oil.

1 Double leg mount the starfish as an extension of one of their arms with a .71 wire. Cut the wire to about 2.5 cm (1 in) and apply florist's adhesive to both the tip of the starfish arm and wire. Push the wired arm into the outside edge of the plastic foam ring. Position all the starfish around the ring. Leave a gap of 3 cm (1¼ in) for attaching the ribbon.

2 Cut the stems of the rose heads to about 2.5 cm (1 in) and put florist's adhesive on their stems and bases. Push the glued stems into the plastic foam to form a ring around its outside edge on top of the starfish. Working towards the centre of the ring, continue forming circles of rose heads until the ring is covered apart from a gap for the ribbon.

3 Pass the ribbon through the centre of the ring and position it so that it sits in the gap between the roses and starfish to cover the foam. This can be used to hang up the wreath or just tied in a bow for decoration.

PEONY AND SHELL DISPLAY
· · ·

This display cleverly mixes sea shells with flowers in a lovely pink, mauve and green arrangement. The result is a beautiful compact dome. The main feature of the display is the beautifully patterned rose-pink conical sea shells which are echoed by the colour and texture of the cracked glazed ceramic container.

MATERIALS
· · ·
knife
· · ·
1 block plastic foam for dried flowers
· · ·
ceramic bowl
· · ·
florist's adhesive tape
· · ·
scissors
· · ·
12 stems dried pale pink peonies
· · ·
3 dried heads hydrangea
· · ·
7 pink conical shells

This arrangement would be perfect for a bathroom, as long as it is not allowed to become too damp.

1 Cut the plastic foam so that it fits snugly into the container and secure it in place with the florist's adhesive tape. Strip the leaves from the peony stems and cut the stems to about 9 cm (3½ in) long. Push the stems into the foam to create a regular dome shape. Arrange the peony leaves liberally throughout the display.

2 Break each hydrangea head into three clusters and push them into the foam, distributing them among the peony heads. Distribute the sea shells throughout the display by pushing their wider bottom ends between the flowers so that they are held in place by the mass of blooms (secure with glue if necessary).

SUMMER DISPLAYS
· · ·

MATERIALS

· · ·

10 stems dried purple larkspur

· · ·

2 pitchers

· · ·

10 stems dried pink larkspur

· · ·

*10 stems blue globe thistle
(small heads)*

· · ·

*10 stems dried green
amaranthus (straight)*

· · ·

*16 stems dried deep pink
peonies*

· · ·

scissors

*Use the displays in a pair to
achieve the maximum impact.*

The majority of people buying fresh summer cut flowers would think of doing no more than informally arranging them in a vase or pitcher of water. These two matching displays in similar pitchers are loosely arranged in what is almost the dried flower equivalent of this informal approach to flower arranging.

The two displays are characterized by their use of summer flowers in typical summer colours: purple and pink larkspur, blue globe thistle, deep pink peonies and green amaranthus.

Creating the displays requires only the most relaxed approach to dried-flower arranging – you just need to consider carefully the visual balance of the materials to their containers.

1 Split the materials into two equal groups. Cut the purple larkspur so that the stems are approximately three times the height of pitchers. Arrange five stems of purple larkspur loosely in each pitcher. Cut the stems of the pink larkspur to a similar length to the purple larkspur.

2 Arrange the pink larkspur in each pitcher. Break off any offshoots on the globe thistle stems to use separately. Cut the main globe thistle stems to three times the height of the pitchers and arrange in each. Separate the offshoots of globe thistle and arrange in each pitcher.

3 Cut the stems of amaranthus to three times the height of the pitchers and arrange five stems in each.

4 Cut the peony stems to different heights, the tallest being 2.5 cm (1 in) shorter than the larkspur, and the shortest being 20 cm (8 in) shorter than the larkspur. Arrange the peonies evenly throughout the other materials.

ROSE AND LEMON NOSEGAY
. . .

MATERIALS
. . .
3 dried lemons with splits in their skin
. . .
.71 wires
. . .
scissors
. . .
15 stems globe thistles
. . .
15 stems dried yellow roses
. . .
twine
. . .
ribbon

Although the lemons have to be wired, this is a simple decoration to make.

Traditionally a nosegay was a small tight bunch of selected herbs, sometimes with flowers, carried about the person, the scent of which was used to combat bad odours and protect against disease. Effectively it was portable pot-pourri. Today the content of a nosegay is just as likely to be chosen for its appearance as its strong aroma.

This nosegay has whole dried lemons, yellow dried roses and blue globe thistles, and is finished with a ribbon tied in a bow. While the roses and lemons have a faint scent, this can be augmented either by steeping the ribbon in cologne or by sprinkling the materials with perfumed oils.

1 Wire the dried lemons by pushing a .71 wire into a split near the base, through the lemon and out of a split on its other side. Bend the wires downwards and twist the two pieces together under the bases of the lemons.

2 Cut the globe thistle and rose stems to approximately 12 cm (4½ in). Start with a dried rose as the central flower and build a small spiralled posy around it by evenly adding the other ingredients.

3 When all the materials have been formed into a tight round posy, tie it with twine at the binding point. Trim the bottom of the stems. Make a ribbon bow and attach it to the binding point.

FLOWER CONE

· · ·

This unusual design employs a series of stacked rings around a cone shape, each ring containing massed flowers of one type and colour to create a quirky display with a strong geometric pattern.

One side of the container is higher than the other so its rim is an ellipse rather than a circle and this is exploited by making the rings of the flowers follow this elliptical shape to form lines of colour sweeping down from back to front.

MATERIALS

· · ·

plastic foam cone for dried
flowers, 28 cm
(11 in) high

· · ·

galvanized metal container,
approximately 11 cm (4½ in)
diameter

· · ·

scissors

· · ·

20 stems dried floss flower

· · ·

40 stems dried pink rose heads

· · ·

20 stems dried marjoram

· · ·

10 stems small dried globe
thistle heads

· · ·

ribbon

1 Wedge the plastic foam cone firmly into the galvanized container. Cut the floss flower stems to about 2.5 cm (1 in) long and arrange a ring around the bottom of the cone to follow the ellipse of the rim of the container. Cut the rose stems to about 2.5 cm (1 in) long and, tight to the first ring, arrange a second ring with the rose heads again following the elliptical shape.

The pretty colours of the display and finishing ribbon make it ideal for a dressing-table where a mirror at its back will show the arrangement in the round.

2 Cut the stems of the marjoram and globe thistle to about 2.5 cm (1 in). Tight to the ring of rose heads, form a third elliptical ring with the marjoram. Tight to the marjoram, form a fourth elliptical ring with the globe thistle. Repeat this sequence of rings until all the cone is covered. At the tip, fix a single rose head.

3 Wrap the ribbon around the galvanized metal container and finish it in a small tied bow at the front of the display.

125

SUMMER TABLE DISPLAY

· · ·

This delicate and pretty little display is designed as a centrepiece for a table laden with summer foods – and whether your dinner party is inside or outside, this display is perfect.

The materials in the arrangement, peach-pink spray roses and pale green honesty and phalaris, combine to create a soufflé of summer colours. Enhance its seasonal feel by sprinkling it with summer scented oil.

1 Cut the plastic foam to fit the basket, so that it projects 2 cm (¾ in) above its rim, and tape it into place using florist's adhesive tape.

2 Take a stem of honesty and cut off the small offshoots of dried seed heads. Use these seed heads on stems cut to about 8 cm (3¼ in), to create a foliage outline.

3 Cut the dried spray roses to a stem length of approximately 8 cm (3¼ in) and arrange them evenly and densely in the plastic foam throughout the honesty.

All the materials have relatively fragile stems which require careful handling, especially when pushing them into the plastic foam.

4 Cut the phalaris stems to a length of about 8 cm (3¼ in) and distribute them evenly throughout the honesty and spray roses.

5 Once all the materials have been used up, tie the ribbon around the basket, finishing it in a bow at the front.

MASSED ARRANGEMENT IN
BLUE AND YELLOW
· · ·

MATERIALS
· · ·

1 galvanized shallow bucket,
30 cm (12 in) diameter
· · ·
2 blocks plastic foam for dried
flowers
· · ·
florist's adhesive tape
· · ·
scissors
· · ·
25 large dyed blue globe thistle
heads
· · ·
35 dried natural heads yellow
achillea

This table decoration would
complement a modern kitchen
or dining-room.

This contemporary arrangement uses simple massed materials in strong contrasting colours to achieve a strikingly bold display. The polished texture of
the silver-grey galvanized bucket provides an ideal visual foundation on which to
build the domed cushion of deep yellow achillea with contrasting spiky, blue
globe thistles.

No special techniques are required to construct the display but you must ensure
the materials are massed to achieve the surface density necessary.

1 Wedge the blocks of foam in place and
tape. Cut the globe thistle stems to
around 12 cm (4¾ in) and arrange in the
foam. Use smaller heads around the
outside and larger heads at the centre.

2 Cut the achillea stems to about 12 cm
(4¾ in) and arrange them between the
globe thistles, massing them carefully so
that no gaps are visible.

GLOBE THISTLE AND MUSSEL SHELL RING

. . .

If you were wondering what to do with all those shells you collected during last year's seaside holiday, this decoration may be the answer. The material content of this display is strongly evocative of the seaside. The spiky globe thistles contrast with the smooth hard surface of the mussel shells, but probably the most memorable feature of the display is its beautiful blue colouring.

MATERIALS
. . .
plastic foam ring for dried flowers, 13 cm (5 in) diameter
. . .
glue gun and glue
. . .
9 half mussel shells
. . .
65 globe thistle heads of various sizes
. . .
scissors

1 Position groups of three slightly overlapping mussel shells at three equidistant points around the ring. Glue them to the plastic foam and to each other, taking great care when using the glue gun which will be very hot.

2 Cut the globe thistle stems to around 2.5 cm (1 in) long, put a small blob of glue on the stem and push them into the plastic foam. Continue this process until all areas of the plastic foam not covered with shells are filled.

The ring would look wonderful displayed in either a bathroom or a kitchen.

SUMMER HAT FRUIT DECORATION

· · ·

To avoid an embarrassing encounter with someone wearing the same hat as you at that wedding or day at the races, create your own unique headwear.

By the addition of the bright summery colours of dried sunflowers, and orange and lemon slices, a plain straw hat is transformed into a millinery masterpiece.

MATERIALS

· · ·

30 dried orange slices

· · ·

.71 wires

· · ·

30 dried lemon slices

· · ·

30 dried apple slices

· · ·

florist's tape (stem-wrap tape)

· · ·

scissors

· · ·

10 dried sunflowers

· · ·

straw hat

· · ·

.32 silver reel (rose) wire

1 Divide the orange slices into groups of three and double leg mount each group on .71 wire. Repeat the process for the lemon and apple slices. Cover the wired stems with florist's tape (stem-wrap tape). Cut the stems of the sunflowers to 2.5 cm (1 in). Double leg mount on .71 wire and cover the wired stems with the tape.

2 Construct a stay wire by grouping together four .71 wires, each overlapping the next by about 3 cm (1¼ in), and taping them together with florist's tape (stem-wrap tape). Continue adding wires until you have reached the required length – approximately 4 cm (1¾ in) longer than the circumference of the crown of the hat.

3 Arrange your wired materials into separate groups for easy access while you work. Tape the individual wired materials on to the stay wire in the following repeating sequence: orange slices; apple slices; sunflower heads and lemon slices. Continue this along the whole length of the stay wire bending it into the shape of the crown of the hat as you work and leaving the last 4 cm (1¾ in) undecorated. Take the undecorated end of the stay wire and tape it to the other end through the flowers.

4 Place the completed garland over the crown of the hat so that it sits on the brim, and stitch in position by pushing lengths of .32 reel (rose) wire through the straw and around the stay wire at four equidistant positions around the hat. Once in position, you may want to adjust the wired elements to achieve the best effect.

The hat decoration is similar to a garland headdress and its construction, although involving wiring, is relatively straightforward.

STARFISH AND ROSE TABLE
DECORATION
· · ·

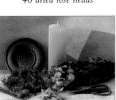

*The cream roses complement
the colour of the candle and
contrast is provided by the
apricot colour and strong
geometric shape of the small
dried starfish.*

This is an alternative decoration for a large church candle using dried rose heads and starfish. The result is a table centre decoration with a seaside feel. This is a simple and quick decoration to make, but is very effective nonetheless.

1 Double leg mount all the starfish individually through one arm with .71 wires to extend their overall length. Cut the wires to approximately 2.5 cm (1 in) in length and put to one side.

2 Position the candle in the centre of the plastic foam ring. Make 2 cm (¾ in) long hairpins from cut lengths of .71 wires. Use these to pin the reindeer moss around the edge of the ring.

3 Group the wired starfish into sets of three and position each group equidistant from the others around the foam ring. Push their wires into the foam to secure.

4 Cut the stems of the dried rose heads to about 2.5 cm (1 in) and push the stems into the foam to form two continuous tightly packed rings of flowers around the candle.

ARTICHOKE PINHOLDER
DISPLAY
· · ·

MATERIALS
· · ·
pedestal stand
· · ·
1 pinholder
· · ·
scissors
· · ·
6 stems contorted hazel
· · ·
9 stems dried artichoke heads
· · ·
*25 stems dried poppy seed
heads*

T his otherwise traditional line arrangement is unusual in that dried materials are used on a pinholder. Dried stems are hard and it is not easy to push them on to the spikes of a pinholder. There is also the heaviness of the artichokes to consider and they have to be carefully positioned to avoid disrupting the physical balance of the arrangement. Make sure that all the stems are firmly pushed on to the pinholder's spikes.

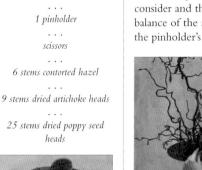

Use naturally trailing stems of hazel at the front of the pinholder and bring it down over the pedestal to the right of its centre line to create a natural trailing effect.

1 Push the hazel stems, cut to 45 cm (18 in) on to the spikes of the pin-holder, positioning the tallest stem at the back.

2 Arrange the artichoke heads throughout the hazel. Use the smallest head on the longest stem centrally at the back. Work away from this with progressively shorter stems. Position the largest artichoke head about two-thirds down from the top of the display.

3 Arrange the poppy seed head stems throughout the display. Position the longest stem at the back, making sure it is shorter than the tallest hazel stem but taller than the tallest artichoke. Work away from this point with progressively shorter stems, with some stems trailing over the front to the right of centre.

SMALL CANDLEHOLDER DISPLAY

• • •

There are many containers in the average household which, because of their colour, shape or material content, are suitable for a flower arrangement. This display was inspired entirely by the small, crown-shaped, brass candleholder in which it is arranged.

An elevated position on, for example, a mantelpiece, would be perfect for such a small, neat display. Indeed, it could be used as a wedding-cake decoration.

MATERIALS

· · ·

knife

· · ·

*1 block plastic foam for dried
flowers*

· · ·

crown-shaped candleholder

· · ·

scissors

· · ·

15 stems poppy seed heads

· · ·

20 stems dried pink roses

1 Cut a piece of plastic foam so that it can be wedged firmly into the candle holder, and sits about 2 cm (¾ in) below its top edge.

2 Cut the stems of the poppy seed heads to 9 cm (3½ in) and push them into the foam, distributing them evenly to create a domed shape.

3 Cut the dried rose stems to 9 cm (3½ in) and push them into the foam between the poppy seed heads, to reinforce the domed outline.

Making the display is straightforward and the method is applicable to any arrangement in a similarly small container.

EDGING BASKET
IN BLUE
· · ·

MATERIALS
· · ·
scissors
· · ·
33 stems globe thistle
· · ·
.71 wires
· · ·
24 stems sea holly
· · ·
.38 silver wire
· · ·
1 bunch floss flower
· · ·
1 bunch marjoram
· · ·
60 stems lavender
· · ·
florist's tape (stem-wrap tape)
· · ·
.32 silver reel (rose) wire
· · ·
*wire-mesh and rectangular
cane basket*

*D*ried flowers transform the
basket into an attractive object
you would happily put on
display in your house.

T ired household containers can be decorated to give them a new
lease of life. This might simply be a fresh coat of paint or, as in
the case of this wire mesh and cane basket, a dried-flower edging
around its rim.

   The display uses the blues and mauves of marjoram, floss flower,
lavender, globe thistle and sea holly to create a decoration with
memorable colour and texture.

1 Cut the globe thistle stems to 2.5 cm
(1 in) long and double leg mount each
with .71 wire. Cut the sea holly stems to
2.5 cm (1 in) and double leg mount each
with .38 silver wire. Split the floss flower
and the marjoram into 20 small clusters of
each on stems 5 cm (2 in) long and double
leg mount them individually with .38
silver wire. Cut the lavender stems to
about 5 cm (2 in) long, group in threes
and double leg mount each group with .38
silver wire. Cover all the wired elements
with florist's tape (stem-wrap tape).

2 Lay a wired stem of sea holly on the edge of the basket and attach it
by binding it in place with a length of .32 silver reel (rose) wire.
Slightly overlap the sea holly with a cluster of floss flower, binding in
place with .32 silver reel (rose) wire. Overlap the floss flower with a
globe thistle head, the globe thistle with the marjoram and the marjoram
with the lavender, binding all of them firmly to the basket with the same
continuous length of reel wire. Repeat the sequence of materials all
around the edge of the basket. When the entire edge of the basket is
covered, stitch the reel wire through the basket several times to secure.

PEONIES AND ARTICHOKES IN AN URN

· · ·

MATERIALS

· · ·

knife

· · ·

*1 block plastic foam for dried
flowers*

· · ·

small cast-iron urn

· · ·

florist's adhesive tape

· · ·

scissors

· · ·

*5 stems dried heads of
flowering artichoke*

· · ·

*8 stems dried pale pink
peonies*

· · ·

*16 stems dried poppy seed
heads*

*The aim of this arrangement
is to show off the attractive
container, so the normal rules
of proportion have been turned
on their head: the vase
accounts for two-thirds of this
arrangement.*

Some containers merit an arrangement specifically designed to show them off and in order to do this, the floral display should neither be too high nor too wide and certainly should not trail down over it.

The particular attraction of this small cast-iron urn is its tall, elegant outline and the grey bloom of its surface. To make the most of the container, the arrangement has been kept low and compact in low-key colours. Pale pink peonies and brown artichokes with purple tufts are set against poppy seedheads with a grey bloom to match the urn.

1 Cut the block of plastic foam so that it can be wedged into the urn level with the rim. Secure the foam in place using florist's adhesive tape.

2 Cut the artichoke stems to about 13 cm (5¼ in). Push one stem into the foam at its centre. Position the other stems around the central stem by pushing them into the foam so that they are slightly shorter, creating a domed outline.

3 Cut the peony stems to about 13 cm (5¼ in) long and push them into the foam evenly and tightly massed throughout but slightly recessed below the artichoke heads.

4 Cut the poppy stems to about 13 cm (5¼ in) long and push them into the plastic foam evenly throughout the artichokes and peonies with their heads level with the artichoke heads.

PEONY AND GLOBE THISTLE CANDLE DECORATION

· · ·

MATERIALS

· · ·

knife

· · ·

*block of plastic foam for dried
flowers*

· · ·

*terracotta pot, 15 cm (6 in)
diameter*

· · ·

wide candle

· · ·

10 dried deep pink peonies

· · ·

*15 stems dried small blue globe
thistle*

· · ·

scissors

*The effect of this display relies
on the peonies being tightly
massed together. Never leave
burning candles unattended
and do not allow the candles to
burn below 5 cm (2 in) of the
display.*

This beautiful arrangement of dried flowers in a terracotta pot is designed to incorporate a candle. Contemporary in its use of massed flowerheads, the display has the stunning colour combination of deep pink peonies and bright blue globe thistles surrounding a dark green candle and finished with a lime-green ribbon. It would make a wonderful gift.

Simple to construct, you could make several arrangements, using different colours and display them as a group. Alternatively, you could change the scale by using a larger container, more flowers and incorporating more than one candle.

1 Cut a piece of plastic foam to size and wedge it firmly into the terracotta pot. Push the candle into the centre of the plastic foam so that it is held securely and sits upright.

2 Cut the peony stems to 4 cm (1½ in) and the globe thistle stems to 5 cm (2 in). Push the stems of the peonies into the foam. Push the stems of the globe thistle into the foam amongst the peonies.

3 Ensure that the heads of all the flowers are at the same level. Wrap a ribbon around the top of the terracotta pot and tie it in a bow at the front. Shape the ends of the ribbon to avoid fraying.

SUMMER POT-POURRI
· · ·

The traditional pot-pourri is based on rose petals because when fresh they have a powerful fragrance, some of which is retained when they are dried, unlike many other perfumed flowers. Today's pot-pourri does not rely entirely on the fragrance of its flowers since there is a wide range of scented oils available and this means materials can be used just for their visual qualities.

This pot-pourri is traditional in that it uses dried roses, but modern in that whole buds and heads have been included instead of petals. The sea holly heads, apple slices and whole lemons are used entirely for their appearance.

1 Break the stems off the lavender leaving only the flower spikes. Place all the dried ingredients in the glass bowl and mix together thoroughly. Add several drops of pot-pourri essence to the mixture of materials – the more you add the stronger the scent. Stir thoroughly to mix the scent throughout the pot-pourri, using a spoon. As the perfume weakens with time it can be topped up by the addition of more drops of essence.

MATERIALS
· · ·
20 stems lavender
· · ·
15 preserved (dried) apple slices
· · ·
5 dried lemons
· · ·
1 handful cloves
· · ·
20 dried pale pink rose heads
· · ·
2 handfuls dried rose buds
· · ·
1 handful hibiscus buds
· · ·
10 sea holly heads
· · ·
large glass bowl
· · ·
pot-pourri essence
· · ·
tablespoon

Predominantly pink and purple, the look and scent of this pot-pourri will enhance any home throughout the summer months.

BATHROOM DISPLAY
· · ·

MATERIALS
· · ·
2 blocks plastic foam for dried
flowers
· · ·
knife
· · ·
pale-coloured wooden trug
· · ·
florist's adhesive tape
· · ·
scissors
· · ·
50 stems natural phalaris
· · ·
40 stems shell-pink roses
· · ·
20 stems cream-coloured
helichrysums
· · ·
150 stems dried lavender
· · ·
15 small dried starfish
· · ·
.71 wires

Though a steamy environment will cause dried flowers to deteriorate, if you accept the shorter life span, such arrangements are an opportunity to add an attractive decorative feature to a bathroom. The starfish in this arrangement evoke images of the sea, whilst the soft pastel colours - shell-pink, apricot, blue, pale green and cream - give it a soft summer look.

Oval shaped, in a rectangular wooden trug, the display is a traditional full arrangement which can be viewed in the round and used anywhere in the house where its pastel shades would look appropriate. The scale and colour of the arrangement is designed to show off the faded blue container.

1 Cut the block of plastic foam to fit the wooden trug and secure it in place with adhesive tape. Cut the individual stems of phalaris to a length of approximately 10 cm (4 in) and push them into the plastic foam to establish the height, width and overall shape of the arrangement.

2 Cut the stems of the dried roses to a length of approximately 10 cm (4 in) and push them into the plastic foam, distributing them evenly throughout.

3 Cut the stems of the helichrysum to a length of about 10 cm (4 in) and push them into the foam amongst the roses and phalaris, recessing some. Cut the dried lavender to 11 cm (4½ in) and, by pushing into the foam, arrange it throughout the display in groups of five stems.

4 Wire all the starfish individually by double leg mounting one of the arms with a .71 wire. Cut the wire legs of the starfish to a length of about 10 cm (4 in) and push the wires into the foam, distributing them evenly throughout the display.

This display involves some wiring but the even distribution of materials helps make it simple to build.

DIAMOND, HEART, SPADE AND CLUB WREATHS

· · ·

These light-hearted wall decorations are instantly recognizable and would make a strong display either grouped together, perhaps in a line, or even individually framed and used separately.

Each decoration uses a single type of material in one colour and has its own distinctive texture. This reinforces the shape of each wreath. The diamond decoration has scented blue lavender spires used directionally to emphasize its simple shape. Appropriately, the heart display incorporates papery-textured red roses. The outline of the spade is formed from pale brown, oval poppy seed heads with distinctive star-shaped crowns and a lovely grey bloom. And bulbous, ribbed nigella seed heads in pale green and burgundy stripes define the shape of the club wreath.

Quite apart from any other consideration, making these decorations is an excellent exercise in taping and wiring techniques. It teaches valuable lessons about the versatility of stay wires in achieving relatively complex shapes, and how the choice of material affects the form of a floral decoration. Begin with the diamond, the simplest of the shapes, and work through the progressively more complex sequence of heart, spade and club and you will encounter an increasing number of factors to take into account to achieve a successful display. It is particularly important to grade the size of materials for both practical considerations, such as decorating difficult corners, and to emphasize features of outline shape.

Making these decorations will increase your understanding and experience of flower arranging and at the same time you will have created unusual and attractive displays.

144

LAVENDER DIAMOND WREATH

· · ·

1 Make a stay wire from .71 wire on which the decoration can be built. Cover with florist's tape (stem-wrap tape). Form the stay wire into a diamond shape about 22 cm (8¾ in) high with the two ends meeting at the bottom point.

MATERIALS

· · ·

.71 wires

· · ·

florist's tape (stem-wrap tape)

· · ·

scissors

· · ·

105 stems dried lavender

· · ·

.38 silver wires

Ensure that all the lavender spires point in the same direction to give this simple wreath maximum impact.

2 Cut the lavender to an overall length of approximately 5 cm (2 in) and group it in threes. Double leg mount these groups with .38 wires, then tape the 35 wired groups with florist's tape (stem-wrap tape).

3 Start at the top point of the diamond shape and attach the groups of lavender by taping around their wired stems and the stay wire. Slightly overlap one group with the next to achieve a continuous line around one half of the shape, finishing at the bottom open end of the stay wire. Start covering the second half of the diamond shape from the bottom open end of the stay wire. When covered, tape the two open ends together.

145

NIGELLA CLUB WREATH
· · ·

MATERIALS

· · ·

.71 wires

· · ·

florist's tape (stem-wrap tape)

· · ·

scissors

· · ·

*57 stems dried nigella seed
heads of similar size*

· · ·

.38 silver wires

*This wreath makes an eye-
catching and fun decoration.*

1 Make a stay wire from .71 wire on which the decoration can be built. Cover with florist's tape (stem-wrap tape). Form the stay wire into a club shape about 22 cm (8¾ in) high with the two ends of the wire meeting in a line at the centre at the bottom of the shape.

2 Cut the stems of the nigella to a length of approximately 2.5 cm (1 in) and double leg mount the individual nigella seedheads on .38 silver wires. Tape the wired stems with florist's tape (stem-wrap tape).

3 Starting at the beginning of the stay wire, tape the wired heads of nigella to the stay wire. Slightly overlap the nigella heads to achieve a continuous line. Continue until the stay wire is covered and then join the two ends of the wire together by taping.

ROSE HEART WREATH

· · ·

MATERIALS

· · ·

.71 wires

· · ·

florist's tape (stem-wrap tape)

· · ·

scissors

· · ·

50 stems dried red roses

· · ·

.38 silver wires

This effective heart would make an unusual and long-lasting Valentine's day gift.

1 Make a stay wire from .71 wire on which the decoration can be built. Cover with florist's tape (stem-wrap tape). Form the stay wire into a heart shape about 22 cm (8¾ in) high with the two ends of the wire meeting at its bottom point.

2 Cut the stems of the dried roses to a length of approximately 2.5 cm (1 in) and double leg mount them individually on .38 silver wires, then tape the wired stems with florist's tape (stem-wrap tape) to hide the wire.

3 Starting at the top, tape the rose stems to the stay wire. Slightly overlap the roses to achieve a continuous line of heads, finishing at its bottom point. Starting back at the top, repeat the process around the other half of the heart. Tape the two ends of the wire together.

POPPY SPADE WREATH
· · ·

MATERIALS
· · ·
.71 wires
· · ·
florist's tape (stem-wrap tape)
· · ·
scissors
· · ·
50 stems dried poppy seed
heads
· · ·
.38 silver wires

*It is important to tape the
poppy seed heads closely
together so that they can rest
against each other and not
"flop" down.*

1 Make a stay wire from .71 wire on
which the decoration can be built.
Cover with florist's tape (stem-wrap tape).
Form the stay wire into a spade shape
about 22 cm (8¾ in) high with the two
ends of the wire meeting in a line at the
bottom of the shape.

2 Cut the stems of the poppy seed heads
to a length of approximately 2.5 cm
(1 in) and double leg mount the
individual poppy seed heads on .38 silver
wires, then tape the wired stems with
florist's tape (stem–wrap tape) to hide
the wire.

3 Starting at the pointed
top of the shape, tape
the poppy seed heads to
the stay wire starting with
the smallest. Slightly
overlap the seed heads to
achieve a continuous line.
The size of the heads
should be increased as you
work towards the bulbous
part of the shape, after
which the heads should be
decreased. When you have
completed one side, repeat
the whole process on the
opposite side, again
starting from the point at
the top. Tape the two ends
of the stay wire together
with tape.

WINTER POT-POURRI
· · ·

The concept of a pot-pourri probably dates from the Elizabethan period when they were used to produce a fragrance to combat the all-pervading bad smells of the times.

This pot-pourri uses its material content in substantial forms – whole oranges, pomegranates, sunflower heads and rose heads with big pieces of cinnamon – because they are included for how they look, not how they smell.

The pot-pourri is mixed using ready-dried materials and although the cloves and cinnamon give it some added spice, it is also worth adding spicy scented oils. A final dusting with gold dust powder gives it a festive Christmas look.

MATERIALS
· · ·
1 handful cloves
· · ·
1 handful dried hibiscus buds
· · ·
1 handful dried tulip petals
· · ·
1 handful small cones
· · ·
7 dried oranges
· · ·
5 dried sunflower heads
· · ·
1 handful dried red rose heads
· · ·
5 small dried pomegranates
· · ·
10 dried grapefruit slices
· · ·
10 cinnamon sticks
· · ·
large glass bowl
· · ·
pot-pourri spicy essence
· · ·
gold dust powder
· · ·
tablespoon

This pot-pourri is very easy to make, so why not have several large bowls of it around the house in winter?

1 Place all the dried ingredients except the cinnamon in the glass bowl and mix together thoroughly. Break the cinnamon sticks into large pieces and add to the mixture.

2 Add several drops of the essence to the mixture. Scatter a tablespoon of gold dust powder over the mixture and stir it well to distribute the gold dust powder and essence throughout the pot-pourri.

EXOTIC ARRANGEMENT

· · ·

MATERIALS

· · ·

1 block plastic foam for dried
flowers

· · ·

knife

· · ·

small cast-iron urn

· · ·

florist's adhesive tape

· · ·

scissors

· · ·

.71 wires

· · ·

handful reindeer moss

· · ·

1 branch contorted willow

· · ·

10 stems Protea compacta
buds

· · ·

15 stems small pink
Protea compacta

· · ·

3 stems Banksia hookerana

· · ·

3 bean stems

· · ·

3 stems Banksia coccinea

*Take care when building the
arrangement because the stems
are hard and will damage the
plastic foam if pushed in and
pulled out too often.*

This display is designed to produce an interesting counterpoint between the unusual floral materials and the traditional way in which they are arranged in a classic cast-iron urn. The rusting surface of the container beautifully complements the brown, pink and orange colouring of the materials.

The forms and textures of the individual contents of the arrangement are strong and hard but the overall effect is softened by the delicate twisting stems of contorted willow which work with the rest of the materials to create harmony within the display.

1 Cut the plastic foam to fit neatly into the urn with a 6.5 cm (2¾ in) projection above its rim. Secure it in place with florist's adhesive tape.

2 Make hairpins from the .71 wires and pin the reindeer moss to the plastic foam around the rim of the urn so that it tumbles over its edge.

3 Establish the overall height, width and fan shape of the arrangement with stems of contorted willow pushed into the plastic foam.

4 Arrange the *Protea compacta* amongst the willow, with the tallest at the back and shorter stems towards the sides and front. Position the *Banksia hookerana* stems in the same way, starting with the tallest at the back.

5 Position the dried bean stems adjacent to the *Banksia hookerana*, reducing their height towards the front. Place the *Banksia coccinea* stems evenly through the display at varying heights.

6 Push the stems of the *Protea compacta* buds into the foam, evenly arranging them throughout the display and decreasing their height from the back to the front and sides.

TEXTURED FOLIAGE RING
· · ·

scissors

· · ·

*10 stems dried natural coloured
honesty*

· · ·

*5 branches glycerine-preserved
beech leaves*

· · ·

*5 branches glycerine-preserved
adiantum*

· · ·

*60 cm (24 in) length dried
hop vine*

· · ·

*twisted wicker wreath ring,
approximately 30 cm (12 in)
diameter*

· · ·

twine

*Very easy to construct from
commercially available
materials, this foliage ring
makes a wonderful autumn
wall decoration for a hall or, if
protected from the weather, a
front door.*

Some types of foliage can be successfully air dried but many others cannot and
need to be glycerine preserved.

This decoration mixes both types of foliage to create a feast of textures and
subtle colours that succeeds without the enhancement of flowers.

1 Cut all the foliage
stems to around 12 cm
(4¾ in) long. You will need
21 lengths of each type of
foliage to cover your ring.
Start by securely tying a
group of three stems of
honesty to the wicker ring
with twine.

2 Making sure it slightly
overlaps the honesty,
bind on a group of three
glycerined beech stems
with the same continuous
length of twine. Repeat
this process with a group
of three stems of hops
followed by a group of
three stems of glycerined
adiantum.

3 Continue binding
materials to the ring in
the same sequence until
the ring is completely
covered. Cut off any
untidy stems and adjust the
materials to achieve the
best effect if necessary.
Finally, tie off the twine in
a discreet knot at the back
of the ring.

WALL HANGING SHEAF

. . .

The rustic charm of this delightful hand-tied sheaf is difficult to resist especially since it is so easy to make once you have mastered the ever-useful stem-spiralling technique.

The focal flowers are large, round, orange globe thistle heads, the hard, spiky geometry of which is set against the creamy-white papery flowers of the helichrysum and country green of linseed and amaranthus. The green carthamus, with its curious orange tufts, acts as a visual bridge between the other materials.

MATERIALS

. . .

1 bunch dried linseed

. . .

1 bunch white helichrysum

. . .

10 stems dried carthamus

. . .

8 stems large dried orange globe thistle

. . .

10 stems dried green amaranthus (straight)

. . .

twine

. . .

scissors

. . .

green paper ribbon

1 Set out the materials so that they are easily accessible. Divide each of the bunches of linseed and helichrysum into 10 smaller bunches. Break off the side shoots from the main stems of the carthamus and the globe thistle to increase the number of individual stems available. Take the longest stem of amaranthus in your hand and, to either side of it, add a stem of carthamus and a bunch of linseed making sure all the material is slightly shorter than the amaranthus. The stems of the materials should be spiralled as they are added. Add materials to the bunch to maintain a visual balance between the bold forms of the globe thistle and helichrysum and the more delicate linseed and carthamus.

The sheaf shape makes a feature of the stems as well as the blooms. Finished with a green ribbon, this decoration would look lovely hung in a country-style kitchen.

2 When all the materials have been incorporated, tie with twine at the binding point. Trim the ends of the stems.

3 Make a paper ribbon bow and attach it to the sheaf at the binding point with its tails pointing towards the flowerheads.

JAM-JAR DECORATIONS
· · ·

MATERIALS
· · ·
3 different-shaped jam jars
· · ·
floral adhesive
· · ·
10 skeletonized leaves
· · ·
scissors
· · ·
18 dried yellow rose heads
· · ·
night-light (tea-light) candles
· · ·
1 bunch dried lavender

Never leave burning candles unattended and do not allow the candle to burn below 5 cm (2 in) of the display height.

Containers decorated with plant materials can be very attractive. This type of external embellishment usually conceals a large part of the container so do not waste money buying special pots and vases, just look around the house for something with an interesting shape that you can use.

Here, three different types and sizes of jam jars are decorated for use as night-light (tea light) holders but they could be used to store pens or bric-a-brac or even in the bathroom for toothbrushes, although the damp will accelerate the deterioration of the materials.

Working on this scale does not use a great deal of material and is an opportunity to use left-over items or materials in some way unsuitable for flower arranging. Use your imagination to vary the type of container and the flower decorations.

1 Apply adhesive to the sides of the tallest jam jar (approximately 12 cm (4¾ in) high) and stick five upward-pointing, slightly overlapping skeletonized leaves around the jar flush with its base. Higher up the jam jar glue on a second layer of five overlapping leaves, slightly offset from the first layer, to cover the joins between the leaves.

2 Cut the stems completely off four dried yellow rose heads and glue them to the leaf-covered jar at four equidistant points around the top of its outer surface. Place a night-light (tea-light) candle in the jar.

3 Cut the stems completely off approximately 14 dried yellow rose heads, apply the floral adhesive to the base of each head and stick them around the neck of the second more squat jam jar. Place them tightly together to form a continuous ring of flowers. Put a night-light (tea-light) in the jar.

4 Paste adhesive on to the outside of the third jam jar. Separate the lavender into single stems and stick them vertically to the side of the jar so that the flower spikes project about 1 cm (½ in) above its rim. The flower spikes should be tight to each other to completely cover the sides of the jam jar. Apply a second layer of lavender spikes lower down so that their flowers cover the first layer of stems. Trim the stems projecting below the jam jar flush with its base. Place a night-light (tea-light) in the jar, or use as a small vase.

These decorations would make an unusual centrepiece to a dining table.

RED DISPLAY IN A
GLASS CUBE
• • •

MATERIALS

20 cm (8 in) glass cube

. . .

20 dried oranges

. . .

knife

. . .

*1 block plastic foam for dried
flowers*

. . .

florist's tape (stem-wrap tape)

. . .

scissors

. . .

2 bunches dried bottlebrush

. . .

*2 bunches dried red-dyed
achillea*

. . .

*2 bunches dried red-dyed globe
thistle*

. . .

2 bunches dried red roses

*The display is easy to make
but clever in that the mechanics
of its construction are hidden
when it is completed.*

This display uses dried oranges to create a coloured base within the glass container itself on which an arrangement using only shades of red is built

The arrangement is a dome of massed materials with contrasting textures: the spikes of globe thistles, the velvet cushions of achillea, and the papery petals of roses. The materials and colours are classical but because of the container used the overall effect is very contemporary.

1 Three-quarter fill the glass cube with dried oranges. Cut the plastic foam block so that it fits into the glass cube snugly above the oranges. Only about a third of the depth of the block should be inside the container. Hold the plastic foam securely in place by taping over it and on to the glass (no more than 2.5 cm/1 in down its sides).

2 Cut the bottlebrush stems to 10 cm (4 in) and create the overall outline of the display by pushing their stems into the plastic foam.

3 Cut the dried achillea to a stem length of 10 cm (4 in) and evenly distribute through the bottlebrush by pushing the stems into the foam.

4 Cut the globe thistle stems to 10 cm (4 in) and position evenly throughout the display, pushing their stems into the foam.

5 Cut the dried rose stems to 10 cm (4 in) in length and, in groups of three, fill the remaining spaces evenly throughout the display.

FIREPLACE ARRANGEMENTS
• • •
MANTELPIECE DISPLAY

MATERIALS
• • •
knife
• • •
*1 block plastic foam for dried
flowers*
• • •
florist's adhesive tape
• • •
string of hops
• • •
5 branches glycerined beech
• • •
3 dried corn cobs
• • •
12 stems dried sunflowers
• • •
*12 stems dried green
amaranthus (straight)*

*Using dried flowers is more
practical than a fresh display
because the arrangement will
last far longer and require little
maintenance.*

When a fireplace is not in use it can lose its status as the focal point of a room but decorating its mantelpiece and grate with dramatic floral arrangements will ensure it remains a major feature. The material contents of this mantelpiece arrangement give it a high summer look; it incorporates bright yellow sunflowers, green amaranthus and green hops with corn cobs used as the focal material.

Construction is relatively straightforward provided you maintain the physical as well as visual balance of the display. So, to prevent the arrangement falling forwards make sure the majority of the weight is kept at the back and, whether the plastic foam is in a tray or sitting directly on the mantelpiece make sure it is firmly secured.

1 Cut the block of plastic foam in half, position one half at the centre of the mantelpiece and secure it in place with adhesive tape. If using a plastic tray, first secure the foam to the tray with adhesive tape, then tape the tray to the mantelpiece.

2 Lie the string of hops along the full length of the mantelpiece and secure it to the ends of the shelf with adhesive tape. The hops on the vine should lie on and around the plastic foam without covering it completely.

3 Push the stems of beech into the plastic foam, distributing them evenly to create a domed foliage outline that also trails into the hops. Push the three stems of the corn cobs into the foam towards the back, one at the centre with a slightly shorter cob at either side.

4 Distribute the sunflowers evenly throughout the plastic foam following the domed shape. Place longer stems toward the back and shorter stems towards the front. Arrange the amaranthus throughout the other materials in the plastic foam to reinforce the outline shape.

FIREPLACE GRATE
ARRANGEMENT
· · ·

*Using dried materials means
that you can make this display
at any time of the year.*

Fill the black hole of an empty grate with a bright display of dried flowers and foliage such as this informal arrangement. The display incorporates the cheery faces of sunflowers with the soft textures of bright green amaranthus and the delicate white flowers of ti tree, all set against the rust tints of beech to create a sunny decoration for a small fireplace.

The plastic foam in this display has been secured by firmly wedging it into the grate. For a larger fireplace the foam will need to be mounted in a separate tray. Do remember that the flowers in a fireplace display are generally arranged to project outwards and preventing it from falling forwards will be the major problem you will encounter.

1 Wedge the plastic foam into the grate. Cut the stems from the branches of glycerined beech and push them into the foam to create a fan-shaped foliage outline that projects out of the grate and forms a curved profile to the front of the display.

2 Push the stems of amaranthus into the foam, distributing them evenly throughout the beech stems to reinforce their outline.

3 Push the sunflower stems into the foam, distributing them evenly throughout the other materials.

4 Push the stems of ti tree in to the foam throughout the display to reinforce the overall shape.

HYDRANGEA CIRCLET
· · ·

Hydrangea heads remain beautiful when dried but they do not necessarily dry well when hung in the air. Thus, while it might seem a contradiction in terms, it is best to dry hydrangea whilst they are standing in shallow water. This slows down the process and avoids the hydrangea florets shrivelling.

There is an enormous range of hydrangea colours, from white through pinks, greens, blues and reds to deep purples and in most cases they keep these colours when dried so are ideal for dried flower arranging.

MATERIALS
· · ·
12 full dried heads hydrangea
· · ·
scissors
· · ·
.71 wire
· · ·
.32 silver reel (rose) wire
· · ·
1 vine circlet, about 35 cm
(14 in) diameter

1 Break down each hydrangea head into five smaller florets. Double leg mount each one individually with .71 wire.

This circlet is a celebration of the colours of dried hydrangeas and the soft, almost watercolour look, of these hues make it the perfect decoration for the wall of a bedroom.

2 Take a long length of .32 silver reel (rose) wire and attach a hydrangea floret to the vine circlet by stitching the wire around one of the vines and the wired stem of the hydrangea, pulling tight to secure. Using the same continuous length of wire, add consecutive hydrangea florets in the same way, slightly overlapping them until the front surface of the vine surface is covered.

3 Finish by stitching the silver reel (rose) wire several times around the vine.

MASSED STAR-SHAPED
DECORATION
· · ·

MATERIALS
· · ·
*2 blocks plastic foam for dried
flowers*
· · ·
knife
· · ·
star-shaped baking tin
· · ·
scissors
· · ·
50 stems dried lavender
· · ·
100 stems dried yellow roses

*The decoration is simple to
make, although it does call for
a substantial amount of
material.*

This display has a huge visual impact of massed colour and bold shape with the added bonus of the delicious scent of lavender.

Built within a star-shaped baking tin and using yellow and lavender colours, the display has a very contemporary appearance. It would suit a modern style interior.

1 Cut the plastic foam so that it fits neatly into the star-shaped baking tin and is recessed about 2.5 cm (1 in) down from its top. Use the tin as a template for accuracy.

2 Cut the lavender stems to 5 cm (2 in) and group them into fives. Push the groups into the plastic foam all around the outside edge of the star shape to create a border of approximately 1 cm (½ in).

3 Cut the dried roses to 5 cm (2 in). Starting at the points of the star and working towards its centre, push the rose stems into the foam. All the heads should be level with the lavender.

FRUIT AND FUNGI BASKET RIM DECORATION

• • •

Creating a dried flower embellishment for the rim of an old and damaged wicker basket gives it a new lease of life by transforming it into a resplendent container for the display of fruit. The decoration is full of the bold textures and rich colours of sunflowers, oranges, lemons, apples and fungi.

MATERIALS

• • •

45 slices dried orange

• • •

45 slices dried lemon

• • •

*45 slices preserved (dried)
apple*

• • •

.71 wires

• • •

18 sunflower heads

• • •

16 small pieces dried fungus

• • •

florist's tape (stem-wrap tape)

• • •

scissors

• • •

*old wicker basket, without a
handle*

• • •

.32 silver reel (rose) wire

1 Group the orange slices in threes and double leg mount each group with .71 wires. Repeat with the lemon and apple slices. Cut the sunflower stems to about 2.5 cm (1 in) and individually double leg mount them on .71 wires. Double leg mount the pieces of fungi with .71 wire. Finally tape over all the wires with florist's tape (stem–wrap tape).

2 Starting at one corner of the basket, bind a group of orange slices to its rim by stitching .32 silver reel (rose) wire through the wicker and around the stem. With the same wire, stitch on the apple slices, the sunflower heads, the lemon slices and the fungi. Repeat this sequence until the rim is covered. Stitch the wire around the last stem and the basket.

The principles of this design can be used to decorate a wicker container of any type.

AUTUMNAL ORANGE DISPLAY
· · ·

MATERIALS
· · ·

*3 blocks plastic foam for dried
flowers*

· · ·

*terracotta pot, 30 cm (12 in)
high*

· · ·

florist's adhesive tape

· · ·

*10 stems glycerine-preserved
adiantum*

· · ·

.71 wires

· · ·

9 dried split oranges

· · ·

scissors

· · ·

10 stems dried carthamus

· · ·

*10 stems orange-dyed globe
thistles*

· · ·

10 stems dried bottlebrush

*This is designed as a feature
display which would be
particularly effective positioned
where it could be viewed in the
round.*

Warm autumn colours dominate this display both in the floral arrangement and in its container. The lovely bulbous terracotta pot is a feature of the display and the arrangement is domed to reflect the roundness of the container. Indeed, in order to focus attention on the pot, the container unusually takes up half the height of the finished display.

The autumnal red and burnt-orange colours of globe thistle, bottlebrush, oranges and adiantum contrast with the green of the carthemus, the orange tufts of which act as a colour link. Texturally varied, the display incorporates tufted flowers, spiky flowers, feathery foliage and recessed leathery skinned fruits.

The arrangement involves simple wiring of the oranges but is otherwise straightforward and just requires a good eye and a little patience in arranging the materials individually in order to achieve the right shape.

1 Pack the blocks of plastic foam into the terracotta pot and secure in place with florist's adhesive tape. The surface of the foam should be about 4 cm (1¼ in) above the rim of the pot.

2 Create a low domed foliage outline using the adiantum stems at their length of about 25 cm (10 in). Wire the dried oranges with .71 wire.

3 Bend down the wires projecting from the bases of the oranges and twist together. Arrange the oranges throughout the adiantum by pushing their wire stems into the foam.

4 Cut the carthamus stems to approximately 25 cm (10 in) and push them into the plastic foam throughout the display to reinforce the height, width and overall shape.

5 Cut the globe thistle stems to a length of approximately 25 cm (10 in) and push them into the foam evenly throughout the display. These are the focal flowers.

6 Finally, cut the stems of bottlebrush to a length of 25 cm (10 in) and push them into the plastic foam to distribute them evenly throughout the display.

DRIED FLOWER TUSSIE
MUSSIES
• • •

MATERIALS
. . .
Tussie Mussie A
scissors
. . .
20 stems dried red roses
. . .
1 bunch dried
Nigella orientalis
. . .
1 bunch dried lavender
. . .
twine
. . .
ribbon
. . .
Tussie Mussie B
scissors
. . .
20 stems dried pink roses
. . .
half bunch nigella seed heads
. . .
half bunch dried lavender
. . .
half bunch phalaris
. . .
twine
. . .
ribbon

*These tussie mussies are easy
to make, although, to achieve a
satisfactory result, they will use
a lot of material in relation to
their finished size.*

These tussie mussies are made of small spiralled bunches of lavender-scented dried flowers. Embellished with embroidered and velvet ribbon bows, they have a medieval look and would make delightful gifts or could be carried by a young bridesmaid.

1 To make Tussie Mussie A, on the right of the main picture, cut all the materials to a stem length of approximately 18 cm (7 in). Set out all the materials in separate groups for easy access. Start by holding a single rose in your hand and add the other materials one by one.

2 Add, in turn, stems of *Nigella orientalis,* lavender and rose to the central stem. Continue this sequence, all the while turning the bunch in your hand to ensure that the stems form a spiral. Hold the growing bunch about two-thirds of the way down the stems.

3 When all the materials are in place, secure the bunch by tying twine around the binding point of the stems. Trim the bottoms of the stems even. Tie a ribbon around the binding point and finish in a neat bow. (Follow the same method for Tussie Mussie B).

Four Seasons in a Basket
· · ·

This contemporary massed display in a circular basket is divided into quarters, each representing - by its material content and colours – one of the four seasons. It is important to keep the materials tightly massed together for maximum effect.

MATERIALS
· · ·
knife
· · ·
2 blocks plastic foam for dried
flowers
· · ·
round shallow basket
· · ·
florist's adhesive tape
· · ·
scissors
· · ·
60 stems dried natural phalaris
· · ·
17 stems cream helichrysum
· · ·
40 dried deep pink roses
· · ·
160 stems dried lavender
· · ·
25 stems carthamus
· · ·
5 stems preserved (dried)
brown adiantum
· · ·
10 cinnamon sticks
· · ·
5 dried oranges with splits
· · ·
.71 wires

1 Cut the plastic foam to fit and wedge it in the basket. Divide the surface of the foam into quarters by making a cross with adhesive tape. Cut the stems of phalaris and helichrysum to a length of about 6 cm (2½ in). Group the phalaris stems in fives and arrange them evenly throughout one quarter of the basket. Distribute the helichrysum among the phalaris with all the heads at the same level.

Cut the stems of the roses to 6 cm (2½ in) and the lavender to an overall length of 7 cm (2¾ in). Group the lavender stems in fives and arrange them in the second quarter of the basket. Push the rose stems into the foam, throughout the lavender.

Cut the stems of carthamus to 6 cm (2½ in). Break fronds of adiantum from the main stems and cut them to 7 cm (2¾ in). Push the carthamus stems into the foam throughout the third quarter of the basket.

Distribute the adiantum evenly among the carthamus, keeping them tight together.

Cut the sticks of cinnamon to 6 cm (2½ in). Single leg mount the dried oranges and cut the protruding wires to a length of 4 cm (1½ in). Push the wires of the oranges into the foam to arrange them evenly throughout the fourth quarter of the basket. Push the cinnamon sticks into the foam, massing them tightly between the dried oranges.

Involving only a small amount of wiring, the display is not difficult to make but is an excellent exercise in massing dried flowers and would make a powerful centrepiece for a circular table.

PINK BASKET
DISPLAY
· · ·

MATERIALS

· · ·

knife

· · ·

*1 block plastic foam for dried
flowers*

· · ·

*oval basket, about 20 cm
(8 in) long*

· · ·

florist's adhesive tape

· · ·

scissors

· · ·

*20 stems dried red amaranthus
(straight)*

· · ·

20 stems dried deep pink roses

· · ·

*20 stems deep pink
helichrysum*

The natural deep pink hues of these
roses, helichrysum and amaranthus
have survived the preservation process
and here work together to produce a
richly-coloured dense textural display
of dried flowers.

The arrangement, mounted in an
oval basket, is a low dome and thus
would be good as a table arrangement,
but its lavish formal appearance would
make it appropriate to any reception
room in the house.

1 Cut the block of plastic foam to fit
snugly into the basket and fix it
securely in place with adhesive tape.

2 Cut the amaranthus to an overall
length of 14 cm (5¾ in) and push
them into the plastic foam to create a
dome-shaped outline.

3 Cut the stems of dried roses to a
length of 12 cm (4¾ in) and push
them into the foam, distributing them
evenly throughout the amaranthus.

4 Cut 10 of the helichrysum stems to approximately 12 cm (4¾ in) in length and push them into the foam evenly throughout the display. Cut the other 10 stems to approximately 10 cm (4 in) in length and push them into the foam evenly throughout the display, so that they are recessed to give visual depth to the arrangement.

The materials in the display have nicely contrasting textures: papery helichrysum, roses and velvet-spiked amaranthus.

CINNAMON AND ORANGE RING

· · ·

MATERIALS

· · ·

glue gun and glue sticks

· · ·

5 dried oranges

· · ·

*plastic foam ring for dried
flowers, 13 cm (5¼ in)
diameter.*

· · ·

20 cinnamon sticks

*This lovely ring would make
an ideal gift – perhaps as a
house-warming present, or for
someone who loves cooking.*

The warm colours, spicy smell and culinary content of this small decorated ring make it perfect for the wall of a kitchen.

The display is not complicated to make but requires nimble fingers to handle the very small pieces of cinnamon used. These pieces have to be tightly packed together to achieve the right effect and great care must be taken because attaching so much cinnamon to the plastic foam may cause it to collapse. To help avoid this happening you can glue the foam ring to stiff card cut to the same outline, before starting work.

1 Apply glue to the bases of the dried oranges and fix them to the plastic foam ring, equally spaced around it. Break the cinnamon sticks into 2-4 cm (¾-1½ in) pieces.

2 Apply glue to the bottom of the pieces of cinnamon and push them into the foam between the dried oranges, keeping them close together to achieve a massed effect.

3 Glue a line of the cinnamon pieces around both the inside and outside edges of the ring to cover the plastic foam completely.

Classic Orange and Clove Pomander

This classic pomander starts as fresh material that, as you use it, dries into a beautiful old-fashioned decoration with a warm spicy smell evocative of mulled wine and the festive season.

Make several pomanders using different ribbons and display them in a bowl, hang them around the house, use them as Christmas decorations or even hang them in your wardrobe.

MATERIALS
· · ·
3 small firm oranges
· · ·
3 types of ribbon
· · ·
scissors
· · ·
cloves

Pomanders are easy and fun to make, and ideal as gifts. Remember to tighten the ribbons as the pomanders dry and shrink.

1 Tie a ribbon around an orange, crossing it over at the base.

2 Finish off at the top of the orange by tying the ribbon into a bow. Adjust the position of the ribbon as necessary to ensure the orange is divided into four equal-sized areas.

3 Starting at the edges of the areas, push the sharp ends of the exposed cloves into the orange skin and continue until each quarter is completely covered.

CLASSICAL URN

· · ·

MATERIALS

· · ·

knife

· · ·

*2 blocks plastic foam for dried
flowers*

· · ·

cast-iron urn

· · ·

florist's adhesive tape

· · ·

scissors

· · ·

10 stems preserved eucalyptus

· · ·

10 stems bleached honesty

· · ·

2 bunches linseed

· · ·

2 bunches natural phalaris

· · ·

20 stems dried white roses

· · ·

1 bunch natural ti tree

A lovely shallow urn in rust-tinged cast iron is the inspiration for
this display. The classic shape of the container is a major feature
of the display and is echoed by a dried flower arrangement of traditional elegance.

Predominantly white and yellow, with contrasting greens, the
display is a dense dome of roses, honesty, ti tree, eucalyptus, linseed
and phalaris.

1 Cut the blocks of
plastic foam to fit into
the cast iron urn and
wedge it in, securing it
with adhesive tape.

2 Cut the eucalyptus
stems to 15 cm (6 in)
long and push them into
the plastic foam to create
an even domed foliage
outline.

3 Cut the honesty stems to about 20 cm
(8 in) in length and push them into
the plastic foam, distributing them
throughout the foliage with longer stems
towards the centre of the urn.

4 Separate the linseed into 18 smaller
bunches, each cut to a length of 15
cm (6 in). Push the bunches into the
plastic foam evenly throughout the other
materials.

The luminosity of the arrangement's pale colours would lighten a dark corner of a room.

5 Cut the phalaris and the rose stems to approximately 15 cm (6 in) in length and individually push into the plastic foam evenly throughout the display.

6 Cut the ti tree stems to approximately 15 cm (6 in) in length and arrange them evenly throughout the display.

RED TIED SHEAF
· · ·

MATERIALS
· · ·
50 stems dried lavender
· · ·
10 stems Protea compacta
buds
· · ·
10 stems natural ti tree
· · ·
15 stems dried red roses
· · ·
twine
· · ·
scissors
· · ·
satin ribbon, 5 cm (2 in)

The demanding aspect of the construction of the sheaf is the technique of spiralling the materials in your hand. But this display is relatively small, which simplifies the task.

A tied sheaf of flowers arranged in the hand makes an attractive and informal wall decoration. To make a successful wall hanging, the sheaf must be made with a flat back, while at the same time it should have a profiled front to add visual interest. With such exotic colours, this is a display that would work best in an interior decorated with rich colours and furnishings.

1 Lay out the materials so that they are easily accessible and separate the lavender into 10 smaller groups. Hold the longest protea in your hand, and behind it add a slightly longer stem of ti tree, then hold rose stems to either side of the protea, both slightly shorter than the first. Continue adding materials in a regular repeating sequence to the growing bunch in your hand, spiralling the stems as you do so.

2 When all the materials have been used, tie the sheath with twine at the binding point. Trim the stems so that they make up about one-third of the overall length of the sheaf.

3 To finish the display make a separate ribbon bow and attach it to the sheaf at the binding point.

ROSE AND CLOVE POMANDER

. . .

This pomander is a decadent display of rose heads massed in a ball. But it has a secret: cloves hidden between the rose heads which give the pomander its lasting spicy perfume.

It relies for its impact on the use of large quantities of tightly packed flowers, all of the same type and colour.

MATERIALS
. . .
ribbon 40 x 2.5 cm
(16 x 1 in)
. . .
.71 wire
. . .
plastic foam ball for dried
flowers, approximately 10 cm
(4 in) diameter
. . .
scissors
. . .
100 stems dried roses
. . .
200 cloves

Almost profligate in its use of materials, this pomander is quick to make and would be a wonderful and very special gift.

1 Fold the ribbon in half and double leg mount its cut ends together with a .71 wire. To form a ribbon handle, push the wires right through the plastic foam ball so that they come out the other end, and pull the projecting wires so that the double leg mounted part of the ribbon becomes firmly embedded in the plastic foam. Turn the excess wire back into the foam.

2 Cut the stems of the dried rose heads to a length of approximately 2.5 cm (1 in). Starting at the top of the plastic foam ball, push the stems of the dried rose heads into the foam to form a tightly packed circle around the base of the ribbon handle. As you work push a clove into the plastic foam between each rose head. Continue forming concentric circles of rose heads and cloves around the plastic foam ball until it is completely covered.

CRESCENT MOON WREATH

· · ·

MATERIALS
· · ·
35 Craspedia globosa *heads*
· · ·
scissors
· · ·
.38 silver wires
· · ·
1 bunch dried linseed
· · ·
florist's tape (stem-wrap tape)
· · ·
.71 wires

This novelty decoration is designed to be hung on the wall of a nursery or child's bedroom. The golden-yellow of *Craspedia globosa* and the pale gold sheen of the linseed seed heads give the decoration a luminosity which children will love.

It is made like a garland headdress, on a stay wire but shaped to the outline of a crescent rather than a circle.

1 Cut the *Craspedia globosa* heads to a stem length of approximately 2 cm (¾ in) and double leg mount them on .38 silver wires. Split the dried linseed into very small bunches, each approximately 4 cm (1¾ in) long, and double leg mount them on .38 wires. Tape all the wired materials with the florist's tape (stem-wrap tape). Create a stay wire about 60 cm (24 in) long from the .71 wire.

2 Cover the stay wire with florist's tape (stem-wrap tape) Bend the stay wire into the outline of a crescent shape, taking care to ensure an even arc and pointed ends.

3 At one open end of the stay wire, tape on a bunch of linseed, followed by a small head of the *Craspedia globosa* slightly overlapping. Use the smaller heads of the *Craspedia globosa* at the pointed ends of the crescent and the larger heads at its centre. As you get towards the centre of the crescent, increase the width of the line of materials by adding material to the sides of the wire. Decrease the width again as you work towards the far point.

4 When the outside edge of the crescent outline has been completed, repeat the process on the inner edge but this time working from the bent point of the crescent down towards the open end of the stay wire. When the inner wire has been decorated, join the two open ends of the stay wire by taping them together, then cut off any excess wires and tape over their ends. This joint will be hidden by the dried materials.

To make the crescent shape accurately – narrower at its points – requires a degree of skill and like all wired decorations, time and patience.

FLOWERS FOR SPECIAL OCCASIONS

· · ·

From a luxurious Valentine's posy of deep red roses and an unusual Christmas wreath of clementines and ivy, to lavish bouquets for birthdays and anniversaries, the calendar year presents wonderful opportunities for the flower arranger. Exciting arrangements for weddings, christenings, Easter and Christmas are featured alongside beautiful floral gift-wrappings for every special occasion.

INTRODUCTION
. . .

*Right: Golden Wedding
Bouquet (page 196)*

Traditionally flowers go hand in hand with special occasions – what would a wedding, a christening or a birthday be without celebratory flowers? Throughout the calendar year, from Valentine's Day to Christmas, the flower arranger has opportunity after opportunity to express his or her creativity.

This usually takes the form of a bunch of flowers, but is nonetheless creative for that, especially if you remember that presentation is all. Cellophane (plastic wrap) or tissue paper gift-wrapping will make even the most simple posy of flowers really special, and attention to details such as tying with ribbon or raffia will pay handsome dividends in its effect.

However, it is the big events like weddings which present the flower arranger with the real challenge. The challenge is not just the need for the necessary skills to design, arrange and wire the materials, but also having the skills to organize the project properly by making a series of important decisions correctly.

*Above: Orchid Corsage
(page 218)*

You must decide exactly what you are going to produce, and calculate the quantities of flowers and foliage necessary. You must avoid buying too much or, worse, buying too little. A carefully considered timetable must be prepared for the event. You must decide when to order the flowers and how long the different varieties will remain in good condition. Remember that some flowers, such as lilies and gladioli, may require a few days before the event to open fully. You must estimate how long it will take to produce each arrangement, headdress and buttonhole. You must consider the time-scale available to you for working with the flowers and, to avoid all-night labouring, how many helpers you will need. Can the large arrangements be made *in situ*, or will they need to be made somewhere else and transported, and if so, how? You must decide what containers, how much plastic foam, and what other sundries you will need.

Clearly, you will need a very long, very comprehensive check-list. And it doesn't even stop there: the participants may wish to have a memento and you will have to consider whether the materials you are using are suitable to preserve. You might even consider the meanings associated with the flowers you are using, so that you can really claim to "say it with flowers".

*Right: Simple Easter
Display (page 187)*

THE MEANINGS OF FLOWER AND HERB NAMES

Acacia	Secret love
Almond blossom	Sweetness, hope
Amaranthus	Immortality
Amaryllis	Pride, splendid beauty
Anemone	Withered hopes, forsaken
Angelica	Inspiration
Apple blossom	Preference
Basil	Good wishes
Bay	Glory
Bellflower (white)	Gratitude
Bluebell	Constancy
Broom	Humility
Buttercup	Childhood

Camellia	Excellence
Carnation	First love
Chives	Usefulness
Chrysanthemum (red)	"I love you"
Clematis	Mental beauty, purity
Coriander (Cilantro)	Hidden worth
Cumin	Fidelity
Daffodil	Deceitful hopes
Daisy	Innocence
Dianthus	Divine love
Evergreen	Life everlasting
Everlasting flower	Unfading memory

Hawthorn blossom	Hope
Heartsease	Remembrance
Hibiscus	Delicate beauty
Holly	Hope, divinity
Honesty	Wealth
Honeysuckle	Devotion
Hyacinth	Loveliness, constancy
Hyssop	Cleanliness
Ivy	Eternal fidelity
Jasmine (white)	Amiability
Jasmine (yellow)	Elegance, happiness
Jonquil	"I desire a return of affection"
Laurel	Triumph, eternity
Lavender	Devotion, virtue
Lemon balm	Sympathy
Lilac (purple)	First emotions
Lilac (white)	Youthful innocence
Lily (white)	Purity
Lily (yellow)	Falsehood, Gaiety
Lily-of-the-valley	Return of happiness
Magnolia	Grief, pride
Marigold	Joy
Marjoram	Blushes
Michaelmas daisy	Farewell
Mint	Eternal refreshment
Mistletoe	Love
Nasturtium	Patriotism

Fennel	Flattery
Forget-me-not	Fidelity, true love
Gardenia	Femininity
Gladiolus	Incarnation

Oak	Forgiveness, eternity
Olive branch	Peace
Orange blossom	Purity, loveliness
Oregano	Substance

Pansies	Love, "Thinking of you"
Parsley	Festivity
Peach blossom	Long life
Peony	Bashfulness
Periwinkle (blue)	Early friendship
Periwinkle (white)	Pleasures of memory
Pinks	Love
Poinsettia	Fertility, eternity
Poppy (red)	Consolation
Rose (red)	Love
Rose (yellow)	Jealousy
Rosebud	Pure and lovely
Rosemary	Remembrance
Rue	Grace, clear vision
Sage	Wisdom, immortality
Salvia (red)	"I am thinking of you"
Snowdrop	Hope, consolation

Sorrel	Affection
Southernwood	Jesting
Stock	Lasting beauty
Sunflower	Haughtiness, false riches
Sweet William	Gallantry
Tansy	Hostile thoughts
Tarragon	Lasting interest
Thyme	Courage, strength
Tulip (red)	Declaration of love
Tulip (yellow)	Hopeless love
Violet	Humility
Wallflower	Fidelity in adversity
Zinnia	"Thinking of absent friends"

FRESH VALENTINE
TERRACOTTA POTS
· · ·

half block plastic foam

· · ·

2 small terracotta pots,
1 slightly larger than the other

· · ·

cellophane (plastic wrap)

· · ·

knife

· · ·

scissors

· · ·

ming fern

· · ·

ivy leaves

· · ·

5 stems 'Santini' spray
chrysanthemums

· · ·

6 stems purple phlox

· · ·

18 dark red roses

Very quick and easy to make,
the simplicity of these charming
decorations is irresistible.

With luck, Valentine's Day brings with it red roses, but these small jewel-like arrangements present them in an altogether different way. The deep red of the roses visually links the two pots: contrasting with the acid lime green of 'Santini' chrysanthemums in one, and combining richly with purple phlox in the other.

1 Soak the plastic foam in water. Line both terracotta pots with cellophane (plastic wrap). Cut the foam into small blocks and wedge into the lined pots. Trim the cellophane to fit. Do not trim too close to the edge of the pot.

2 Build a dome-shaped foliage outline in proportion to each pot. In the larger pot, push the stems of ming fern into the plastic foam and in the small pot push the ivy leaves into the foam.

3 In the larger pot, arrange 'Santini' chrysanthemums amongst the ming fern. In the small pot, distribute the phlox amongst the ivy to emphasize the dome shapes of both.

4 Strip the leaves from the dark red roses, cut the stems to the desired lengths and arrange evenly throughout both displays.

SMALL FRESH ROSE
VALENTINE'S RING
· · ·

While this delightful floral circlet could be used at any time of the year, the impact created by the massed red roses makes it particularly appropriate to Valentine's Day. It can be hung on a wall or, with a candle at its centre, used as a table decoration for a romantic dinner for two.

MATERIALS
· · ·
plastic foam ring,
15 cm (6 in) diameter
· · ·
dark green ivy leaves
· · ·
.71 wires
· · ·
bun moss
· · ·
20 dark red roses
· · ·
scissors

If you receive a Valentine's Day bouquet of red roses, why not recycle them? After the rose blooms have fully blown open, cut down their stems for use in this circlet to extent their lives. Finally dehydrate the circlet and continue to use it as a dried flower display.

1 Soak the plastic foam ring in water. Push individual, medium-sized ivy leaves into the foam to create an even foliage outline all around the ring.

2 Make hairpin shapes out of the .71 wires and pin small pieces of bun moss on to the foam ring between the ivy leaves. Do this throughout the foliage but to a thinner density than the ivy.

3 Cut the rose stems to approximately 3.5 cm (1½ in) long and push them into the foam until the ring is evenly covered. The ivy leaves should still be visible in-between the rose heads.

DRIED VALENTINE
DECORATION IN A BOX
· · ·

MATERIALS
· · ·

*1 block plastic foam
(for dried flowers)*

· · ·

knife

· · ·

heart-shaped box

· · ·

scissors

· · ·

1 bunch dried red roses

· · ·

2 bunches dried lavender

· · ·

*2 bunches dried poppy seed
heads*

· · ·

1 bunch Nigella orientalis

*This arrangement is easy to
make, but to get the best effect
you must not scrimp on
materials. The flowerheads
need to be massed together very
tightly to hide the foam.*

This display, in a heart-shaped box, demonstrates that dried flowers and seed heads look very striking and attractive when massed in groups of one type. Filled with romantic roses and scented lavender, this display can be made as a gift for Valentine's Day or simply as a treat for yourself. It can also be made at any other time of year using a different-shaped box.

1 Stand the block of plastic foam on its end and carefully slice in half down its length with a knife. Then shape both pieces, using the box as a template, so that they will each fit into one half of the box. Fit these two halves into the heart-shaped box ensuring that they fit snugly.

2 Divide the heart shape into quarters, separating each section by a line of the materials to be used. Fill one quarter with rose heads, one with lavender, one with poppy seed heads and the last with *Nigella orientalis*. Make sure that all the material heads are at the same level.

VALENTINE'S HEART CIRCLET

Instead of the traditional dozen red roses, why not give the love of your life a wall hanging decoration for Valentine's Day?

Set your heart (in this case wooden) in a circlet of dried materials full of romantic associations – red roses to demonstrate your passion, honesty to affirm the truth of your feelings and lavender as sweet as your love.

MATERIALS

· · ·

33 dried red rose heads

· · ·

scissors

· · ·

.38 silver wire

· · ·

florist's tape (stem-wrap tape)

· · ·

55 stems dried lavender

· · ·

10 stems dried honesty

· · ·

.71 wires

· · ·

1 small wooden heart, on a
string

This takes a little more effort than ordering a bunch of flowers from your florist, but that effort will be seen as a measure of your devotion.

1 Cut the dried rose stems to approximately 2.5 cm (1 in) and individually double leg mount on .38 silver wires, then cover the stems with tape. Group three rose heads together and double leg mount on .38 wire, then cover the stems with tape. Repeat the process for all the rose heads, making in total eleven groups.

Group the dried lavender into bunches of five stems and double leg mount on .38 silver wire, then tape. Repeat the process for all the lavender stems, making in total eleven groups.

Cut individual pods from the stems of dried honesty and group into threes, double leg mounting them together on .38 silver wires and taping. Make eleven groups in total.

Make a stay wire from .71 wires.

2 Lay a group of the honesty pods over one end of the stay wire and tape on securely. Then add, so that they just overlap, a group of lavender stems followed by a group of rose heads, taping each group to the stay wire. Keep repeating this sequence, all the while bending the stay wire into a circle.

3 When the circle is complete, cut off any excess stay wire leaving approximately 3 cm (1¼ in) to overlap. Then tape the two ends together through the dried flowers to secure. Tie the string from the wooden heart on to the stay wire between the dried blooms, so that the heart hangs in the centre of the circlet.

CHILDREN'S PARTY PIECES
. . .

MATERIALS
. . .
1 block plastic foam
. . .
knife
. . .
3 enamel mugs
. . .
scissors
. . .
*24 pink and yellow
"mini-gerbera"*

*The gerbera's sugary colouring
means the display can be
integrated with the contents of
the table – surround them with
jelly and blancmange or have
them emerging from a
mountain of sweets!*

Most people probably think that flowers are wasted on a children's party, but if we can make them fun, then why not?

Gerbera are extraordinary in their simple form and bright colours, and look like a child's idea of a flower. In this display the gerbera are arranged upright and apparently unsupported in simple containers, just like a child's drawing.

1 Soak the block of plastic foam in water. Using a knife, cut small pieces of foam and wedge them into the bottom of each mug so that they take up about one third of the depth.

2 Cut the gerbera stems so that they are approximately 5 cm (2 in) taller than the mug. Push the stem ends into the foam, keeping the flowers upright and pushing some in further than others to get slight variations of height.

SIMPLE EASTER DISPLAY
· · ·

This display strips away all embellishments and relies entirely on the intrinsic beauty of the flowers themselves for its impact. To heighten the impact, the flowers are massed in one type only in each container.

The displays are appropriate to Easter because they use familiar flowers which are associated with spring and convey the message of rebirth.

MATERIALS
· · ·
50 stems pale blue grape
hyacinth
· · ·
1 tea-cup
· · ·
scissors
· · ·
4 pale pink 'Angelique' tulips
· · ·
2 pitchers (1 larger than the
other)
· · ·
15 mauve crocus flowers
· · ·
30 stems of narcissi (some
cream, some white)
· · ·
2 jam jars

1 Measure the grape hyacinth against the tea-cup and cut their stems so that only the heads can be seen above the rim. Also cut the 'Angelique' tulip stems so that only the heads project above the rim of the smaller pitcher. Again, cut the crocus stems so that only their flowerheads are visible above the rim of the larger pitcher. Four tulip heads is sufficient for this small display.

2 Trim the narcissi stems so that the overall height of the flowers is twice the height of the jar. Loosely arrange a mixture of both varieties in each jar. By using a variety of containers the finished display has a good variation of height.

The displays can be grouped together or used individually around the house. They are simple to make, but remember simplicity is often the essence of good design!

EASTER WREATH

. . .

MATERIALS

. . .

*plastic foam ring,
30 cm (12 in) diameter*

. . .

elaeagnus foliage

. . .

scissors

. . .

5 polyanthus plants

. . .

8 pieces of bark

. . .

.71 wires

. . .

3 blown eggs

. . .

2 enamel spoons

. . .

70 stems daffodils

. . .

raffia

*Whether in the church or
home, this delightful Easter
decoration will bring pleasure
to all who view it.*

Easter is a time of hope and regeneration and this bright Easter wreath visually captures these feelings. It overflows with the floral symbols of spring with daffodils and polyanthus, and contains eggs, a symbol of birth.

The vibrant colours and the flowers, arranged to look as though they are still growing, give the wreath a fresh, natural glow. There is also a touch of humour in the crossed enamel spoons.

1 Soak the foam ring in water and arrange an even covering of elaeagnus stems, approximately 7.5 cm (3 in) long, in the foam. At five equidistant positions, add groups of three polyanthus leaves.

3 Arrange the polyanthus flowers in single-coloured groups as though they are growing by pushing their stems into the plastic foam. Be sure to leave a section of the ring clear for the eggs and spoons. Cut the daffodils to a stem length of approximately 7.5 cm (3 in) and between four groups of polyanthus arrange groups of 15 daffodils, pushing their stems into the plastic foam.

2 Wire the eight pieces of bark by bending a .71 wire around the middle and twisting to achieve a tight grip. Position the pieces of bark equidistant around the ring by pushing the protruding wires into the plastic foam.

4 Bend .71 wires around the spoons and twist. In the gap left on the ring position one of the spoons, wrapping the wire ends around to the back of the ring. Twist the wires together tightly so that the spoon is embedded in the foam. Do this with both spoons, arranged so that they cross. Wrap raffia around the eggs, crossing it over underneath and tying it on the side. Bend .71 wires around the eggs, twisting the ends together gently. Arrange the remaining daffodils and polyanthus flowers around the eggs and spoons.

RUBY WEDDING DISPLAY

· · ·

Designed as a table arrangement complete with celebratory bow around its container, this display of rich and passionate colours would be a magnificent gift.

Formal looking, but simple in its construction, this Ruby Wedding arrangement is a lavish mass of deep purple tulips and velvet red roses set against the dark glossy green of camellia leaves. A beautiful paper bow completes the effect.

1 Approximately three-quarters fill the bowl with water. Cut the stems of camellia and roses to 7.5 cm (3 in) longer than the depth of the container. Arrange the camellia stems in the bowl to create a low domed foliage outline within which the flowers will be arranged. Arrange half the roses evenly throughout the camellia.

2 Cut the tulip stems to approximately 7cm (3 in) longer than the depth of the bowl and strip away any remaining lower leaves from the stems. Position the tulips in the display, distributing them evenly throughout the roses and camellia. Finally add the remaining roses evenly throughout the arrangement to complete a dense, massed flower effect of deep red hues.

3 Form a festive bow from the paper ribbon. The bow should be substantial but it is important that it is kept in scale with the display. To complete the arrangement tie the bow to the container so that it sits on the front.

BABY BIRTH GIFT
· · ·

1 block plastic foam

· · ·

scissors

· · ·

small galvanized metal bucket

· · ·

1 bunch Pittosporum

· · ·

*15 stems pale pink
'Angelique' tulips*

· · ·

5 stems white spray roses

· · ·

10 stems white ranunculus

· · ·

10 stems white phlox

· · ·

1 bunch dried lavender

· · ·

*ribbon, purple and white check
(plaid)*

*The choice of soft subtle
colours means it is suitable for
either boy or girl. There is also
the added bonus of the
beautiful scents of the phlox
and dried lavender.
Since the arrangement has its
own container it is particularly
convenient for a recipient in
hospital, avoiding, as it does,
the need to find a vase!
Finally, the container can be
kept and used after the life of
the display.*

Celebrate a baby's birth by giving the parents this very pretty arrangement in an unusual but practical container. The display incorporates double tulips, ranunculus, phlox and spray roses, with small leaves of *Pittosporum*. It is the delicacy of the flowers and foliage which make it appropriate for a baby.

1 Soak the plastic foam in water, cut it to fit the small metal bucket and wedge it firmly in place. Cut the *Pittosporum* to a length of 12 cm (4¾ in) and clean the leaves from the lower part of the stems. Push the stems into the plastic foam to create an overall domed foliage outline within which the flowers can be arranged.

2 Cut the 'Angelique' tulips to a stem length of 10 cm (4 in) and distribute them evenly throughout the foliage. Cut individual off-shoots from the main stems of the spray roses to a length of 10 cm (4 in), and arrange throughout the display, with full blooms at the centre and buds around the outside.

3 Cut the ranunculus and phlox to a stem length of 10 cm (4 in) and distribute both throughout the display. Cut the lavender to a stem length of 12 cm (4¾ in) and arrange in groups of three stems evenly throughout the flowers and foliage. Tie the ribbon around the bucket and finish in a generous bow.

PLANTED BASKET FOR BABY

. . .

This display of pot plants in a basket makes a lovely gift to celebrate the birth of a baby. It is easy to make and quick to prepare, and is a long-lasting alternative to a cut flower arrangement.

MATERIALS

. . .

1 wire basket

. . .

2 handfuls Spanish moss

. . .

cellophane (plastic wrap)

. . .

scissors

. . .

*3 pots miniature white
cyclamen*

. . .

3 pots lily-of-the-valley

. . .

paper ribbon

*The combination of two
simple and delicate white
plants, baby cyclamen and lily-
of-the-valley, gives the design
charm and purity, indeed
everything about it says
"baby".*

1 Line the wire basket with generous handfuls of Spanish moss, then carefully line the moss with cellophane (plastic wrap). Trim the cellophane to fit around the rim of the basket.

2 Remove the plants from their pots carefully. Loosen the soil and the roots a little before planting them in the basket, alternating the cyclamen with the lily-of-the-valley.

3 Make sure that the plants are firmly bedded in the basket. Make two small bows from the paper ribbon and attach one to each side of the basket at the base of the handle.

DRIED FLOWER HORSESHOE BABY GIFT

· · ·

MATERIALS
· · ·
14 heads dried, white roses
· · ·
42 heads dried, bleached honesty
· · ·
60 heads dried phalaris grass
· · ·
scissors
· · ·
.38 silver wire
· · ·
florist's tape (stem-wrap tape)
· · ·
.71 wires
· · ·
ribbon

What could be nicer for new parents than to receive a floral symbol of good luck on the birth of their baby?

The whites and pale green of this dried flower horseshoe make it a perfect gift or decoration for the nursery.

1 Cut the rose stems, honesty stems and phalaris grass to approximately 2.5 cm (1 in) long. Double leg mount the roses individually on .38 silver wire, then tape. Double leg mount the phalaris heads in groups of five on .38 silver wire, and the honesty in clusters of three on .38 silver wire. Tape each group.

2 Make a stay wire approximately 30 cm (12 in) long from .71 wire on which the horseshoe will be built.

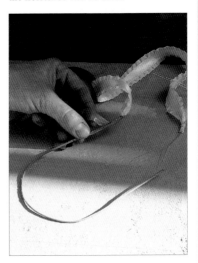

3 Form three small bows approximately 4 cm (1½ in) wide from the ribbon and bind them at their centres with .38 silver wire. Cut a 30 cm (12 in) length of ribbon and double leg mount both ends separately with .38 silver wire. This will form the handle for the horseshoe.

4 Form the stay wire into a horseshoe shape. Tape one wired end of the ribbon to one end of the stay wire. Tape one of the bows over the junction of the ribbon and stay wire, making sure it is securely in place.

5 Starting at the bow, tape the flowers and foliage to the stay wire, to its mid point, in the following repeating sequence: phalaris, rose, honesty. Tape a bow at the centre and tape the last bow and the remaining ribbon end to the other end of the stay wire. Work the flowers in the same sequence back to the centre point.

While making the horseshoe is relatively time-consuming, the effort will no doubt have created something of such sentimental value that it will be kept forever.

GOLDEN WEDDING
BOUQUET
· · ·

MATERIALS
· · ·
*20 stems golden yellow
ranunculus*
· · ·
20 stems mimosa
· · ·
gold twine
· · ·
scissors
· · ·
*2 sheets gold-coloured tissue
paper in 2 shades*
· · ·
*piece gold-coloured fabric
approx. 46 cm (18 in) long,
15 cm (6 in) wide*
· · ·
gold dust powder

*This arrangement makes a
flamboyant gift but nonetheless
is as simple to create as a
hand-tied bouquet. It can be
unwrapped and placed straight
into a vase of water, with no
need for further arranging.*

This shimmering bouquet makes an unequivocal Golden Wedding statement. Unashamed in its use of yellows and golds, the colours are carried right through the design in the flowers, the wrapping paper, the binding twine and the ribbon, even to a fine sprinkling of gold dust powder.

1 Lay out the stems of ranunculus and mimosa so that they are easily accessible. Clean the stems of leaves from about a third of the way down. Holding a stem of ranunculus in your hand, start to build the bouquet by adding alternate stems of mimosa and ranunculus, turning the flowers in your hand all the while so that the stems form a spiral.

2 When all the flowers have been arranged in your hand, tie the stems together at the binding point with the gold twine. When secured, trim the stems to a length approximately one-third of the overall height of the bouquet.

3 To wrap the bouquet, lay the two shades of tissue on top of each other and lay the bouquet diagonally on top. Pull up the sides of the paper, then the front, and hold these in place by tying the gold twine around the binding point. To complete the display, tie the gold fabric around the binding point and create a bow. Scatter a little gold dust powder over the flowers. Separate the sheets of tissue to give a fuller appearance.

CUT FLOWERS AS A GIFT

· · ·

MATERIALS

· · ·

*10 stems cream French
tulips*

· · ·

*6 branches lichen-covered
larch twigs*

· · ·

scissors

· · ·

10 stems calla lily

· · ·

raffia

· · ·

cellophane (plastic wrap)

*Because it is a spiral-tied
bouquet it can be placed
straight into a container
without the need for further
arranging.*

T his elegant, long-stemmed bouquet is the gift for a very special occasion. This is a cool and uncluttered arrangement in which the cream colours and soft surfaces of calla lilies and French tulips are brought into focus by the coarse textures and irregular shapes of lichen-covered larch twigs. As a finishing touch, the bouquet is wrapped in cellophane (plastic wrap) and tied with raffia in a bow.

1 Set out all materials for easy access. Remove the lower leaves from the tulip stems and cut the larch twigs to a more manageable length.

Start with a calla lily and add twigs and tulips, all the while turning the growing arrangement so that the stems form a spiral.

2 Continue adding stems and larch twigs until all the materials are used. Tie securely at the binding point with raffia. Trim level the stem ends of the completed bouquet, taking care to avoid cutting them too short.

3 Cut a large square of cellophane (plastic wrap) and lay the bouquet diagonally across it. Wrap the cellophane up around the sides of the bouquet to overlap at the front. Tie securely at the binding point and finish with a raffia bow.

FRESH FLOWERS AS A
GIFT-WRAP DECORATION
• • •

This is essentially a corsage used to decorate a wrapped gift. It offers the opportunity to make the gift extra special, and to give flowers at the same time. The colour and form of the gerbera and 'Mona Lisa' lily heads are very bold, and this is contrasted with the small delicate bell heads of lily-of-the-valley and lace-like grey lichen on the larch twigs.

MATERIALS
• • •
1 stem lily 'Mona Lisa'
• • •
scissors
• • •
1 branch lichen-covered larch
• • •
1 small pot lily-of-the-valley
• • •
2 pink gerbera
• • •
raffia
• • •
gift-wrapped present
• • •
ribbon

The decoration is made as a small, tied, flat-based sheaf. This involves no wiring and thus is relatively simple to make, provided you give sufficient thought to the visual balance between the bold and delicate elements.

1 From the lily stem, cut a 20 cm (7¾ in) length with one bud and one open flower on it. Also cut a single open flower on an 8 cm (3¼ in) stem. Cut six twigs from the larch branch, each about 25 cm (10 in) long. Cut three lily-of-the-valley on stems approximately 15cm (6 in) long, each with a leaf.

Cut one gerbera stem to 18 cm (7 in) long and the second to 14 cm (5½ in) long. Create a flat fan-shaped outline with the lichen-covered larch twigs. Position the longer lily stem in the centre of the fan and the single lily head immediately below.

Next arrange the lily-of-the-valley and gerbera flowerheads around the two open lilies. Tie the stems securely with raffia at the point where they all cross (the binding point).

2 Lay the completed decoration diagonally across the wrapped gift and take a long piece of raffia around it, crossing underneath the parcel and bringing it back up to tie off on top of the stems.

Tie the ribbon around the binding point of the decoration and form it into a bow.

DRIED FLOWERS AS A GIFT-WRAP DECORATION

· · ·

MATERIALS

· · ·

1 dried sunflower head

· · ·

scissors

· · ·

.71 wires

· · ·

1 small dried pomegranate

· · ·

*3 small pieces dried fungi
(graded in size)*

· · ·

*3 slices dried orange
(graded in size)*

· · ·

.38 silver wires

· · ·

*florist's tape
(stem-wrap tape)*

· · ·

gift-wrapped present

· · ·

raffia

*It takes a little time to produce
but its natural, warm, earthy
colours make this a delightful
enhancement well worth the
effort, and something to keep.*

To make a present extra special why not make the wrapping part of the gift? The construction of this display is effectively a dried flower corsage but used to embellish gift wrapping.

1 Cut the sunflower to a stem length of 2.5 cm (1 in) and double leg mount on a .71 wire. Single leg mount the pomegranates on .71 wire. Double leg mount the small pieces of fungi on .71 wires and the orange slices on .38 silver wires.

2 Wrap all the wired materials with tape, then attach the three orange slices to one side of the sunflower and pomegranate, then attach the three layers of fungi on the other side. Bind all these in place using the .38 silver wire.

3 Trim the wire stems to a length of 5 cm (2 in) and tape together with florist's tape (stem-wrap tape). Tie the raffia around the present and push the wired stem of the decoration under the raffia knot. Secure in place with a .71 wire.

DRIED FLOWERS AS A GIFT
· · ·

This is a great way to present dried flowers as a gift. Treat them as you would a tied bunch of cut fresh flowers – make an arranged-in-the-hand, spiral-stemmed bouquet that can be placed straight into a vase.

MATERIALS
· · ·
10 small dried pink Protea
compacta buds
· · ·
10 stems dried pink larkspur
· · ·
10 stems dried pink peonies
· · ·
10 stems dried green
amaranthus
· · ·
raffia
· · ·
scissors
· · ·
2 sheets blue tissue paper
· · ·
pink ribbon

The deep pink mixture of exotic and garden flowers – protea and amaranthus with peonies and larkspur – makes this a floral gift anyone would be thrilled to receive.

1 Lay out the dried materials so that they are all easily accessible. Start the bouquet with a dried protea held in your hand, add a stem of larkspur, a stem of peony and a stem of amaranthus, all the while turning the growing bunch.

2 Continue until all the dried materials have been used. Tie with raffia at the binding point – where the stems cross each other. Trim the stem ends so that their length is approximately one-third of the overall height of the bouquet.

3 Lay the sheets of tissue paper on a flat surface and place the bouquet diagonally across the tissue. Wrap the tissue paper around the flowers, overlapping it at the front. Tie securely at the binding point with a ribbon and form a bow.

OLD-FASHIONED GARDEN ROSE TIED BRIDESMAID'S POSY

· · ·

MATERIALS
· · ·
*5 deep red and 5 pale apricot
rose heads on stems*
· · ·
scissors
· · ·
20 stems mint
· · ·
6 vine leaves
· · ·
twine
· · ·
raffia

*Finished with a natural raffia
bow, the posy has a fresh, just-
gathered look. Happily, it is
very simple to make.*

This tiny hand-tied posy of blown red and pale apricot roses and mint is designed to accompany the bridesmaid's circlet headdress. The velvet beauty of the contents gives it charm and impact.

1 Remove all thorns and lower leaves from the rose stems. Starting with a rose in one hand, add alternately two stems of mint and one rose stem until all the materials are used. Keep turning the posy as you build to form the stems into a spiral. Finally add the vine leaves to form an edging to the arrangement and tie with twine at the binding point.

2 Trim the ends of the stems so that they are approximately one-third of the overall height of the posy. Tie raffia around the binding point and form it into a secure bow.

CIRCLET HEADDRESS FOR A
YOUNG BRIDESMAID
• • •

Although classic in its design, this bridesmaid's circlet headdress is given a contemporary feel by the use of a rich colour combination not usually associated with traditional wedding flowers.

MATERIALS
· · ·
*9 individual deep red rose
heads*
· · ·
*9 small clusters apricot
spray roses*
· · ·
8 small bunches rosehips
· · ·
scissors
· · ·
.71 stub wires
· · ·
9 small individual vine leaves
· · ·
.38 silver wires
· · ·
9 small bunches mint
· · ·
florist's tape (stem-wrap tape)

*The small bunches of orange-
red rosehips give a substance to
the fabric-like texture of the red
and apricot coloured roses.*

1 Cut all the flowers to a stem length of approximately 2.5 cm (1 in). Wire the individual rose heads with .71 wires. Stitch wire the vine leaves with .38 silver wire. Tape all the wired items.

Make the stay wire with .71 wires approximately 4 cm (1½ in) longer than the circumference of the head. Tape the wired flowers and foliage to the stay wire in the following repeating sequence: individual rose, mint, spray rose, vine leaf, rosehips. As you tape materials to the stay wire, form it into a circle. Leave 4 cm (1½ in) of the stay wire undecorated, overlap it behind the beginning of the circlet and tape securely together through the flowers.

Tied Bridal Bouquet

. . .

MATERIALS

. . .

10 stems Lilium
longiflorum

. . .

10 stems cream-coloured
Eustoma grandiflorum

. . .

10 stems white
Euphorbia fulgens

. . .

5 stems Molucella laevis

. . .

10 stems white aster
'Monte Cassino'

. . .

10 stems dill

. . .

10 ivy trails

. . .

twine

. . .

scissors

. . .

raffia

*To create a bouquet of this
size requires quite a large
quantity of materials which
may prove expensive, but the
design lends itself to being
scaled down to suit a tighter
budget by using the same
materials in smaller quantities.*

This classic "shower" wedding bouquet has a generous trailing shape and incorporates *Lilium longiflorum* as its focal flowers, using the traditional, fresh bridal colour combination of white, cream and green.

Because the flowers are left on their stems the bouquet is physically quite heavy; however, visually, the arrangement has a natural, loose appearance with the long, elegant stems of *Euphorbia fulgens* and asters emphasizing the flowing effect.

1 Lay out your materials so that they are easily accessible. Hold one stem of *Lilium longiflorum* in your hand about 25 cm (10 in) down from the top of its flower head. Begin adding the other flowers and ivy trails in a regular sequence to get an even distribution of materials throughout the bouquet. As you do this, keep turning the bunch in your hand to make the stems form a spiral.

3 When you have finished the bouquet and are satisfied with the shape, tie it with twine at the binding point, firmly, but not too tightly. Cut the stems so that they are 12 cm (4¾ in) long below the binding point. Any shorter and the weight of the bouquet will not be distributed evenly and it will make it difficult to carry.

2 To one side of the bouquet add materials on longer stems than the central flower – these will form the trailing element of the display. To the opposite side add stems slightly shorter than the central bloom, and this will become the top of the bouquet. Spiralling the stems will enable the short, upper part of the bouquet to come back over the hand when it is being carried. This will ensure a good profile, which is essential to avoid it looking like a shield.

4 Tie raffia around the binding point and form a bow which sits on top of the stems, facing upward towards the person carrying the bouquet.

SCENTED BRIDESMAID'S BASKET

· · ·

MATERIALS

· · ·

small basket

· · ·

cellophane (plastic wrap)

· · ·

scissors

· · ·

quarter block plastic foam

· · ·

knife

· · ·

florist's adhesive tape

· · ·

ribbon

· · ·

.38 silver wires

· · ·

20 10 cm (4 in) stems golden privet

· · ·

6 stems tuberose

· · ·

20 stems 'Grace' freesias

A very young bridesmaid will find it much easier to carry a basket than clutch a posy throughout what must seem an endless wedding ceremony.

This basket uses simple flowers, in a simple colour combination, simply arranged. The result is a beautiful display appropriate for a child.

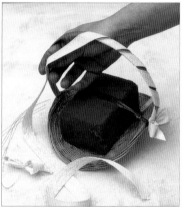

1 Line the basket with cellophane (plastic wrap) to make it waterproof. Trim the cellophane edges to fit. Soak the quarter block of plastic foam in cold water, trim to fit into the basket and secure in a central position with florist's adhesive tape.

2 Form two small bows from the ribbon. Tie around their centres with .38 silver wires and leave the excess wire projecting at their backs. Bind the handle of the basket with ribbon securing it at either end by tying around with the wire tails of the bows.

3 Build a slightly domed outline throughout the basket with the golden privet, cut to the appropriate length.

4 Cut the tuberose stems to about 9 cm (3½ in) and position in a staggered diagonal across the basket.

5 Cut the freesia stems to approximately 9 cm (3½ in) long and distribute evenly throughout the remainder of the basket. Recess some heads to give greater depth to the finished display.

The wonderful scent of tuberose and freesia is a great bonus to this delightful display.

SCENTED GARLAND
HEADDRESS
· · ·

MATERIALS
· · ·
12 small stems golden privet
· · ·
.38 silver wires
· · ·
scissors
· · ·
12 small clusters mimosa
· · ·
12 small clusters crab apples
· · ·
12 heads freesia 'Grace'
· · ·
12 heads tuberose
· · ·
florist's tape (stem-wrap tape)
· · ·
.71 wires

Making the headdress is time consuming and requires a degree of wiring skill, but the result will be well worth the effort. And, of course, it can be kept after the event, although as the flowers are quite fleshy you will need to use the silica gel method of drying.

This garland headdress just oozes the colours and scents of summer: yellows and cream hues mix with the perfumes of tuberose, freesia and mimosa.

The design of the garland allows the headdress simply to sit on the head of the bride or bridesmaid with no need for complex fixing to the hair.

1 Cut the stems of privet to 5 cm (2 in) and double leg mount with .38 silver wire. Cut the mimosa and crab apple stems to 5 cm (2 in) and, grouping them in separate clusters, double leg mount with .38 silver wire. Wire the freesia and tuberose heads on .38 silver wire using the pipping method, and then double leg mount on .38 silver wire. Tape all the wired materials.

2 With .71 wire make a stay wire approximately 4 cm (1 in) longer than the circumference of the bride's or bridesmaid's head – this extra length will remain undecorated.

3 Tape the materials on to the stay wire in the following sequence: privet, tuberose, mimosa, crab apples and freesia. Curve the stay wire into a circle as you proceed.

4 To finish the headdress neatly, overlap the undecorated end of the stay wire with the decorated beginning. Tape the wires together, through the flowers, to secure.

YELLOW ROSE BUTTONHOLE

• • •

The bold choice of vibrant colours characterizes this stunning buttonhole. The yellow roses and elaeagnus, the orange red rosehips and lime green fennel combine to produce a simple, visually strong decoration suitable for either a man or a woman.

MATERIALS

· · ·

scissors

· · ·

1 yellow rose

· · ·

.71 wires

· · ·

*5 elaeagnus leaves, graded in
size*

· · ·

.38 silver wires

· · ·

15 rosehips and leaves

· · ·

1 head fennel

· · ·

florist's tape (stem-wrap tape)

· · ·

.32 silver reel (rose) wire

· · ·

pin

As with all buttonholes, the construction involves wiring which is, of course, time consuming. Make sure you leave plenty of time to create buttonholes on the morning of the ceremony.

1 Cut the rose stem to 4 cm (1½ in) and wire on .71 wire. Stitch wire all the elaeagnus leaves with .38 silver wires. Group the rosehips, on stems of 4 cm (1½ in), in bunches of five and wire with .38 silver wires. Divide the head of fennel into its component stems and wire in groups with .38 silver wires. Tape all the wired elements.

2 Keeping the rose head central to the display, bind the bunches of fennel and rosehips around it, with .32 silver reel (rose) wire. Bind the elaeagnus leaves to the arrangement with .32 silver reel (rose) wire, placing the largest leaf at the back of the rose, the two smallest at the front, and two medium sized leaves at the side.

3 Trim the wires to approximately 7 cm (2½ in) and tape the wires with florist's tape (stem-wrap tape). Look closely at the completed buttonhole, and, if necessary, bend the leaves down to form a framework for the rose, and adjust the overall shape so that the back of the decoration is flat for pinning to the lapel.

NERINE HAIR COMB

· · ·

*Quite intricate to construct,
this decoration will take
practice before you get it right.*

This beautiful hair decoration, built on a comb, is suitable for the bride who finds a circlet too cumbersome. Delicate in form, but strong in colour, the comb headdress incorporates a variety of textures and colours; bright pink nerines, pink tinged hydrangeas and berries in shades of pink.

1 "Pip" the flowerheads and buds from the main nerine stem. Wire the open nerine florets by passing a bent .38 silver wire with a loop at its end down the throat of the bloom, so that the loop wedges in the narrowest part. Double leg mount each wired flowerhead, the nerine buds and the individual hydrangea florets with .38 silver wires. Cover the stems of all the wired elements with florist's tape (stem-wrap tape).

2 Make two units of nerine with one bud at the top and one slightly open bloom below it. Make two units of two hydrangea florets.

3 Take the two nerine units and bind them together approximately 2 cm (¾ in) below the junction of the stems using the .32 silver reel (rose) wire. Bind the units of hydrangea florets to the nerine units with the .32 wire. Bend both units back to form a straight line, with the nerines slightly longer than the comb and the hydrangea florets slightly shorter.

4 Position an open nerine bloom at the centre of these bound units, with the top of the flower about 5 cm (2 in) above the binding. This is the focal flower. Add the individual flowers and buds to reinforce the shape. Secure them at the binding point with .32 silver reel (rose) wire. Secure the berries at the binding point with .32 silver reel (rose) wire.

Decorative, without being cumbersome, this hair comb makes an eye-catching adornment for a bride's head.

5 When the decoration is complete, separate the wire stems below the binding point into two equal groups and bend them back on themselves parallel to the main stems. Trim the wires at an angle to thin them out, cover each group of wires with tape, to create two prongs.

6 Lay these two wire prongs along the flat back of the comb and tape in position by passing the tape through the teeth in the comb and around the wire prongs. Do this all the way along the length of the comb until the decoration is securely attached.

DRIED FLOWER HAIR COMB

. . .

MATERIALS

. . .

scissors

. . .

*7 dried yellow
rose heads*

. . .

9 dried phalaris heads

. . .

.38 silver wires

. . .

3 small dried starfish

. . .

9 short stems eucalyptus

. . .

*5 heads dried, bleached
honesty*

. . .

*florist's tape
(stem-wrap tape)*

. . .

plastic hair comb

*This hair comb is quite
intricate to construct but can be
made in advance of the event,
and the materials are, of
course, available all year round.*

A decorated hair comb is an alternative headdress to the circlet and is particularly useful if the hair is worn up. This decoration in dried flowers is almost monochromatic, with creamy white roses, silvery-grey eucalyptus, silvery-white honesty and soft green phalaris, with the colourful apricot-coloured dried starfish. The starfish also provide strong graphic shapes, which contrast with the softness of the flowers to create a stunning effect.

1 Cut the rose heads and the phalaris to a stem length of 2 cm (¾ in) and double leg mount them with .38 silver

wires. Double leg mount the small starfish with .38 silver wire. Cut two of the eucalyptus stems to a length of 6 cm (2¼ in) and the rest to about 4 cm (1½ in). Double leg mount all the eucalyptus and individual heads of honesty with .38 silver wire. Cover the wired stems of all the materials with florist's tape (stem-wrap tape). Create six units, two containing two roses, two with two phalaris and two with two eucalyptus stems, one at 6 cm (2¼ in) and one at 4 cm (1¼ in), with the longer stem at the top of the unit.

2 Take two eucalyptus units and bind them together about 2 cm (¾ in) below the junction of the stems using .38 silver wire. At the binding point, bend each of two wired units away from each other to form a straight line slightly longer than the length of the comb. Take all the units of rose and phalaris heads and bind them individually to the eucalyptus unit at the binding point and bend each of them flat in the same way. Make all of these units slightly shorter than the eucalyptus.

3 Place an individual rose head at the centre of the bound units with the top about 5 cm (2 in) above the binding point. This will be the focal flower. Position the starfish and the honesty around this central rose head and secure at the binding point with .38 silver wire. Position the individual heads of phalaris and short stems of eucalyptus so that they reinforce the shape and profile of the decoration. Bind all items in place with .38 silver wire.

As well as making an attractive hair decoration, this hair comb can be kept as a momento of a very special day.

4 Next, separate the wire stems below the binding point into two equal groups of wires, bend them apart and back on themselves, parallel to the main stems. Trim the wires at an angle to thin them out before covering each group of wires with tape to create two wired prongs.

5 Lay these two wire prongs along the top of the comb and tape into position by passing the tape between the teeth in the comb and around the wire prongs. Do this all the way along the length of the comb until the decoration is securely attached.

CHURCH PORCH
DECORATION
• • •

MATERIALS

• • •

gloves

• • •

secateurs

• • •

20 bunches long ivy trails

• • •

twine

• • •

6 large branches rosehips

• • •

raffia

• • •

scissors

This type of decoration is hard work but if you really go for it, the result will be spectacular.

Church festivals, weddings and christenings offer the flower arranger an opportunity to work on a large scale by decorating the church porch. To be successful, the display must have dramatic impact, although it can be simple in its material content.

This porch decoration is designed to look natural, almost as though it is growing out of the structure. Flowers would have been lost in the green mass of ivy, so colour contrast is provided by branches of red rosehips (branches of seasonal blossom would also have the necessary visual strength).

1 Generously drape the ivy trails over the supporting beam of the porch roof starting from the outsides and working towards the centre. As you drape the ivy over the beam, secure at regular intervals with twine.

2 Continue draping the ivy until the beam is evenly covered. Then, again, starting from the outsides, position the branches of rosehips on the top of the ivy trails to hang over the front of the porch.

3 Firmly secure the branches of rosehips in position with twine. Finally form a large bow with the raffia and attach it to the central vertical strut above the rosehips and ivy.

OLD-FASHIONED GARDEN ROSE WEDDING CORSAGE

· · ·

MATERIALS

· · ·

8 stems rose leaves

· · ·

scissors

· · ·

3 rose heads graded thus: in bud, just open, fully open

· · ·

3 small vine leaves

· · ·

.38 silver wires

· · ·

florist's tape (stem-wrap tape)

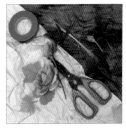

Using just one type of flower with its own foliage and three individual leaves ensures the result is simple yet elegant.

This delicate rose corsage would provide the perfect finishing touch for that special wedding outfit. However, it is best to remember that old-fashioned garden roses are really only available in the summer months.

1 Cut the stems of the rose leaves to length thus: two at 6 cm (2¼ in), two at 4 cm (1½ in), four at 3 cm (1⅛ in). Cut the rose head stems to 4 cm (1½ in). Cut the vine leaf stems to 2.5 cm (1 in) and stitch

wire with .38 silver wire.

Make two "units" of rose leaves each with one 6 cm (2¼ in) stem and one 4 cm (1½ in) stem. Make a "unit" using the two smaller rose heads.

Hold one unit of rose leaves in your hand and place the unit of rose heads on top so that the leaves project slightly above the upper rose head. Bind the units together with .38 silver wire, 6 cm (2¼ in) below the lower rose head.

Add the second unit of rose leaves lower and to

the left of the first. Add the fully opened rose (the focal flower) with the top of its head level with the bottom of the rose above. Bind to the corsage.

Position the vine leaves around the focal flower and bind in place. Position the remaining individual rose leaves slightly recessed around the focal flower and bind in place.

Trim off the ends of the wires approximately 5 cm (2 in) below the focal flower and cover with tape. Adjust as desired.

WEDDING BASKET

· · ·

It has long been a tradition that female guests at weddings are given a "gift" to take home with them. These often take the form of a silk tulle bag containing pastel-coloured sugar almonds.

This symbolically romantic heart-shaped basket is decorated with fresh flowers so that it can be used as a container for such gifts.

MATERIALS

· · ·

scissors

· · ·

10 heads white alstromeria
'Ice cream'

· · ·

10 heads white ranunculus

· · ·

10 heads white spray rose
'Princess'

· · ·

10 clusters small,
white phlox buds
'Rembrandt'

· · ·

.38 silver wires

· · ·

1 bunch pittosporum

· · ·

florist's tape (stem-wrap tape)

· · ·

1 heart-shaped basket
(loose weave)

· · ·

.32 silver reel (rose) wire

1 Cut all the flowerheads and foliage to a stem length of approximately 2.5 cm (1 in). Double leg mount all the flowers and foliage with one or two .38 silver wires, depending on the weight of each flowerhead. You will need about 25 small, wired stems of pittosporum foliage. Tape all the wired elements with florist's tape (stem-wrap tape). Lay out your materials, ready to decorate the basket one side at a time.

Placed on each table at the wedding reception and filled with sugar almonds, the basket will also make a very attractive decoration in itself.

2 Lay a stem of pittosporum at the basket's centre. Stitch .32 silver reel (rose) wire through the basket and over the pittosporum stem. Stitch a bud of alstromeria over the foliage, followed by a rose head, more pittosporum, a ranunculus head and a cluster of phlox.

3 Repeat this sequence until you reach the bottom point, then stitch .32 silver reel (rose) wire through the basket weave to secure. Decorate the other side of the heart basket, this time working in the opposite direction. Again secure with .32 silver reel (rose) wire.

ORCHID CORSAGE

· · ·

MATERIALS
· · ·
*7 orchid flowerheads (spray
orchids)*
· · ·
.38 silver wires
· · ·
*5 small Virginia
creeper leaves*
· · ·
10 stems of bear grass
· · ·
.71 wire
· · ·
*florist's tape
(stem-wrap tape)*
· · ·
scissors

*The corsage is relatively
intricate to make, but the effort
required is rewarded with a
particularly stylish accessory.*

Orchids tend to be naturally ostentatious flowers and as such are perfect for wedding corsages. The grandeur of the spray orchids make them particularly suitable for the mothers of the bride and groom.

1 Double leg mount the orchid heads individually with .38 silver wires. Stitch wire the Virginia creeper leaves by passing a .38 silver wire through the leaflets and bending the wire down to form a false stem, double leg mount this

and whatever natural stem exists with another .38 silver wire. Taking two stems of bear grass, bend them into a loop with a tail, double leg mount this on a .71 wire. Make a total of five bear-grass loops, then tape all of the wired materials.

2 Hold a wired orchid head between your index finger and thumb, add a wired leaf, then bind these together approximately 4 cm (1 in) down the wired stem using the .38 silver wire. Add the rest of the materials creating a very small wired posy, binding them in place with the .38 silver wire. Make sure that the binding point remains in one place.

3 When positioning the materials ensure that the looped bear grass is evenly distributed and that the leaves are also arranged in a regular way through the design so that it is evenly balanced.

4 When everything is wired in place trim the wire stems to about 5 cm (2 in) and cover with florist's tape (stem-wrap tape). Once completed, you may wish to gently manoeuvre the individual elements to achieve the most satisfactory effect.

This stunning corsage can add an element of glamour to even the simplest of clothing.

YELLOW ROSE
BRIDESMAID'S BASKETS
· · ·

MATERIALS
· · ·
FOR EACH BASKET YOU
WILL NEED:

half block plastic foam
· · ·
knife
· · ·
1 small basket (plastic lined)
· · ·
scissors
· · ·
30 stems birch,
approximately 10 cm
(4 in) long
· · ·
10 stems yellow roses
· · ·
5 stems fennel
· · ·
raffia

The flowers are secured in
plastic foam and will stay fresh
for the bridesmaid to keep after
the wedding.

These arrangements will keep young bridesmaids happy on two counts; first they're easier to carry than posies and second the simple bright colours are such fun – sunshine yellow roses and lime-green fennel in a basket stained orange-red.

1 Soak the plastic foam in water, cut it to wedge in the basket.(If you are using a shallow basket, you may need to secure the foam in place with florist's adhesive tape.)

2 Clean the leaves from the bottom 3 cm (1½ in) of the birch stems, then arrange them in the plastic foam creating an even domed outline.

3 Cut the roses and fennel to a stem length of 8 cm (3¼ in) and distribute them evenly throughout the birch stems.

4 Tie a raffia bow at the base of the handle on both sides and trim to complete the display.

Yellow Rose Bridesmaid's Posy

• • •

A posy made from slim-stemmed materials has a narrow binding point which makes it easier to carry. This posy uses such materials in a simple but striking combination of yellow roses, lime-green fennel and delicate green birch leaves.

MATERIALS
• • •
20 stems yellow roses
• • •
5 stems fennel
• • •
15 stems birch leaves
• • •
twine
• • •
scissors
• • •
raffia

1 Strip all but the top 15 cm (6 in) of the rose stems clean of leaves and thorns. Split the multi-headed stems of fennel until each stem has one head only. This makes them easier to handle and visually more effective. Strip all but the top 15 cm (6 in) of the birch stems clean of leaves.

Easy to make as a hand-held, spiralled bunch and finished with a natural raffia bow, this posy would be a delight for any bridesmaid to carry and enjoy.

2 Holding one rose in the hand, add individual stems of fennel, birch and rose in a continuing sequence, all the while turning the bunch to spiral the stems. Continue until all the materials are used.

3 Tie the posy with twine at the point where the stems cross – the binding point. Trim the bottom of the stems to leave a stem length of approximately one-third of the overall height of the finished display.

4 Complete the posy by tying raffia around the binding point and finishing with a bow. Finally, trim the ends of raffia.

CELEBRATION TABLE
DECORATION
• • •

MATERIALS
· · ·
plastic foam ring,
40.7 cm (16 in) diameter
· · ·
scissors
· · ·
12 stems Senecio laxifolius
· · ·
15 stems elaeagnus
· · ·
3 groups 2 chestnuts
· · ·
.71 wires
· · ·
thick gloves
· · ·
18 stems yellow roses
· · ·
10 stems cream-coloured
Eustoma grandiflorum
· · ·
10 stems solidago
· · ·
10 stems dill

*The arrangement is based on
a circular, plastic foam ring
with the centre left open to
accommodate the wine cooler.
The splendid silver wine cooler
is enhanced by the beauty of
the flowers, and in turn its
highly polished surface reflects
the flowers to increase their
visual impact.*

A table for any celebratory lunch will not usually have much room to spare on it. In this instance there is no room for the wine cooler, and the answer is to incorporate this large, but necessary piece of catering equipment within the flower arrangement.

The floral decoration is a sumptuous, textural display of gold, yellow and white flowers with green and grey foliage. The spiky surfaces of the chestnuts add a wonderful variation in texture.

1 Soak the plastic foam ring in water. Cut the senecio to a stem length of around 14 cm (5½ in) and distribute evenly around the ring, pushing the stems into the plastic foam, to create an even foliage outline. Leave the centre of the ring clear.

2 Cut the elaeagnus to a length of about 14 cm (5½ in) and distribute evenly throughout the senecio to reinforce the foliage outline, still leaving the centre of the plastic foam ring clear to eventually accomodate the wine cooler.

3 Double leg mount three groups of two chestnuts on .71 wire and cut the wire legs to about 6 cm (2¼ in). Take care, as the chestnuts are extremely prickly and it is advisable to wear heavy duty gardening gloves when handling them.

4 Still wearing your gloves, position the groups of chestnuts at three equidistant points around the circumference of the plastic foam ring, and secure by pushing the wires into the plastic foam.

5 Cut the rose stems to approximately 14 cm (5½ in) in length and arrange in staggered groups of three roses at six points around the ring, equal distances apart, pushing the stems firmly into the plastic foam.

6 Cut stems of eustoma flowerheads 12 cm (4¾ in) long from the main stem. Arrange the stems evenly in the foam. Cut the stems of solidago to a length of about 14 cm (5½ in) and distribute throughout. Finally cut the stems of fennel to about 12 cm (4¾ in) long and add evenly through the display, pushing the stems into the plastic foam.

This magnificent arrangement would make a stunning centrepiece for a wedding table.

DRIED FLOWER GARLAND HEADDRESS

· · ·

*An advantage of using dried
materials is that they can be
made well in advance, which
means less to worry about on
the big day. There is plenty of
wiring involved, but otherwise
the construction is relatively
straightforward.*

This wedding headdress is made from dried materials in beautiful soft pale pinks, greens and lilacs with the interesting addition of apple slices. Apart from being very pretty, it will not wilt during the wedding and can, of course, be kept after the event.

1 Cut the peonies and the roses to a stem length of 2.5 cm (1 in). Double leg mount the peonies with .71 wires and the roses with .38 silver wires. Group the roses into threes and bind together using the .32 silver reel (rose) wire. Group the apple slices into threes and double leg mount them together with .71 wire. Cut the sprigs of ti tree, hydrangea clusters and eucalyptus to lengths of 5 cm (2 in) and double leg mount with .38 silver wires, grouping the ti tree and eucalyptus in twos. Cover all the wired stems with tape.

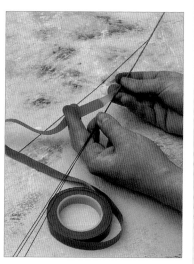

2 Have to hand the bride's head measurements. Make the stay wire on which the headdress will be built with .71 wires, ensuring its final length is approximately 4 cm (1½ in) longer than the circumference of the head.

3 Position a piece of wired eucalyptus on one end of the stay wire and wrap florist's tape (stem-wrap tape) over its stem and the stay wire, to secure them together. Then, in the same way, add in turn a hydrangea cluster, a group of roses, a peony and a group of ti tree, repeating the sequence until the stay wire is covered. Remember to leave the last 4 cm (1½ in) of the stay wire uncovered.

4 To complete the headdress, overlap the uncovered end of the stay wire with the decorated start and tape together with florist's tape (stem-wrap tape), ensuring the tape goes under the flowers so that it is not visible.

The bold nature of this headdress makes it particularly suitable for a bride.

DRIED POMANDER

. . .

MATERIALS

. . .

scissors

. . .

*10 stems glycerined
eucalyptus*

. . .

*plastic foam ball for dried
flowers, 15 cm (6 in) diameter*

. . .

3.5 cm (1¼ in) wide ribbon

. . .

.71 wire

. . .

30 stems dried pink roses

. . .

.38 silver wire

. . .

florist's tape (stem-wrap tape)

. . .

*12 stems dried pale pink
peonies*

. . .

*12 preserved (dried) apple
slices*

. . .

1 sprig dried ti tree

*This pomander is time
consuming to build, but will
last. Sprinkle pot pourri
oil over it to provide a
continuing aroma.*

A pomander is generally defined as a ball of mixed aromatic substances. However, this pomander is designed more for its visual impact than its scent. It would look particularly attractive if carried by a bridesmaid. Alternatively it can be hung in the bedroom, perhaps on the dressing-table.

1 Cut the eucalyptus stems into approximately 10 cm (4 in) lengths. Make sure that the stem ends are clean and sharp, and carefully push them into the plastic foam, distributing them evenly over its surface.

2 Cut a length of ribbon long enough to make a looped carrying handle. Make a loop in the ribbon and double leg mount the two cut ends together on .71 wire. Push the wire firmly into the plastic foam ball to form the carrying handle.

3 Cut the stems of the dried roses to approximately 4 cm (1½ in) and wire individually with .71 wire. Group together in threes and bind with .38 silver wire and cover with tape. Cut the dried peony stems to approximately 4 cm (1½ in) and wire them individually on .71 wire, then tape. Wire the dried apple slices individually on .71 wire.

4 Push the wired peonies into the plastic foam, distributing them evenly all over the ball. Push the wired apple slices into the foam, also distributing them evenly over the ball.

5 Push the ten groups of wired roses into the foam, distributing them evenly all over. Cut the ti tree stems into 9 cm (3 in) lengths and push into the foam to fill any gaps around the ball. Once completed you may wish to gently reposition individual elements in order to achieve the most pleasing effect.

Younger bridesmaids may find this charming ball easier to carry than a posy.

DRIED FLOWER CORSAGE

· · ·

MATERIALS

· · ·

scissors

· · ·

2 dried peonies

· · ·

3 dried peony leaves

· · ·

.71 wire

· · ·

.38 silver wire

· · ·

3 slices preserved (dried) apple

· · ·

3 sprigs dried ti tree

· · ·

3 small clusters hydrangea

· · ·

8 dried roses

· · ·

*3 short stems preserved
(dried) eucalyptus*

· · ·

raffia

· · ·

*florist's tape
(stem-wrap tape)*

· · ·

.32 silver reel (rose) wire

*As an alternative to wearing
the corsage, it could be attached
to a handbag or a prayer book.
Of course, it can be kept after
the event and perfumed with
scented oil*

If dried flowers are the choice for a wedding, a corsage as magnificent as this would be perfect for the mother of the bride. This floral decoration is characterized by softly faded colours in a variety of textures. Dried peonies are used as the focal flowers supported by hydrangeas, roses, ti tree and eucalyptus, and given contrasting textural substance by the unusual addition of preserved apple slices.

1 Cut the peony stems to 4 cm (1½ in) and the three peony leaves to 10 cm (4 in), 8 cm (3¼ in) and 6 cm (2¼ in) respectively. Double leg mount all of these with .71 wire, apart from the shortest peony leaf, which is double leg mounted with .38 silver wire. Double leg mount the apple slices with .71 wire. Cut the sprigs of ti tree to 5 cm (2 in) and form into three small groups, then repeat the process with the hydrangea florets and double leg mount with .38 silver wire.

Cut the rose stems to a length of 2.5 cm (1 in) and the eucalyptus to a length of about 4 cm (1½ in) and double leg mount both on .38 silver wire. Make a small raffia bow and double leg mount on a .38 silver wire around its centre. Tape all of the wired elements with tape ready for making up.

2 Taking the peonies, roses, apple slices and peony leaves, gradually build the arrangement, securing each item individually with .32 silver reel (rose) wire.

3 Position the remaining elements. Attach the raffia bow by its wired stem at the bottom of the arrangement. Secure all materials in place with the .32 silver reel (rose) wire.

4 Trim the ends of the wires to around 6 cm (2¼ in) and cover with tape. You may wish to adjust the wired components to achieve your desired shape.

DRIED ROSE AND APPLE BUTTONHOLE

· · ·

There are several reasons why dried flowers are preferred for some weddings. This might be because the bride wishes to keep her flowers after the event or it may be a practical measure for a winter wedding where fresh flowers are unavailable or expensive. This buttonhole is designed for a groom or best man and, unusually, incorporates fruit with the flower and foliage.

1 Double leg mount the apple slices together on .71 wire. Wire each rose, with a 2.5 cm (1 in) stem, on .71 wire. Double leg mount three roses on .38 silver wire. Leave a 5 cm (2 in) stem on the eucalyptus and hydrangea and double leg mount on .38 silver wire. Tape all the elements.

2 Hold the rose heads in your hand and place the apple slices behind. Then position the hydrangea to the left and bind together all the stems using .32 silver wire. Position the eucalyptus stems to frame the edge of the buttonhole and bind with .32 silver wire.

3 When all these elements are bound securely in place, cut the wired stems to a length of approximately 5 cm (2 in) and bind them with florist's tape (stem-wrap tape). Adjust the wired components to achieve your desired shape, not forgetting the profile.

MATERIALS

· · ·

3 slices preserved (dried) apples

· · ·

.71 wires

· · ·

scissors

· · ·

6 dried roses

· · ·

.38 silver wire

· · ·

6 short stems glycerined eucalyptus

· · ·

1 small head dried hydrangea

· · ·

florist's tape (stem-wrap tape)

· · ·

.32 silver reel (rose) wire

Apple slices give texture and a light touch to the decoration. Add a few drops of rose oil to give scent.

BRIDE'S VICTORIAN POSY WITH DRIED FLOWERS

· · ·

Traditionally the Victorian posy, be it dried or fresh, took the form of a series of concentric circles of flowers. Each circle usually contained just one type of flower, with variations only from one circle to the next. Such strict geometry produced very formal-looking arrangements particularly suitable for weddings.

1 Cut the roses and peonies to a stem length of 3 cm (1⅛ in) and individually single leg mount them on .71 wires. Cut the eucalyptus stems to 10 cm (4 in) and remove the leaves from the bottom 3 cm (1⅛ in), then wire as for roses and peonies.

Double leg mount the phalaris grass and honesty heads on .38 silver wire in groups of five. Single leg mount these groups on .71 wires to extend their stem lengths to 25 cm (10 in). Repeat the process with groups of linseed and hydrangea.

All wired elements should be taped with florist's tape (stem-wrap tape).

2 Hold the central flower, a single white rose head, in your hand and arrange the three peony heads around it, then bind together with .32 silver reel (rose) wire, starting 10 cm (4 in) down the extended stems. (Remember that the starting point for binding determines the final size of the posy, and all subsequent flower circles must be bound at the same point.)

3 Rotating the growing posy in your hand, form a circle of pink rose heads around the peonies and bind to the main stem. Around this, form another circle, this time alternating white rose heads and clusters of hydrangea, and bind. Each additional circle of flower heads will be at an increasing angle to the central flower to create a dome shape.

4 Next add a circle of phalaris grass to the posy. followed by a circle of alternating honesty heads and linseed. Bind each circle with .32 silver reel (rose) wire at the binding point.

The design of this bride's posy follows the Victorian method with just a degree of latitude in the content of some circles. Of course, the arrangement is time-consuming to produce, but the reward is a beautiful posy that the bride can keep forever.

5 Finally add a circle of eucalyptus stems and bind. The eucalyptus leaves will form a border to the posy and cover any exposed wires underneath.

6 To form a handle, place the bundle of bound wires diagonally across your hand and trim off any excess wires. Tape with florist's tape (stem-wrap tape) and cover the handle with ribbon.

DRIED GRASS HARVEST SWAG

· · ·

MATERIALS

· · ·

*1 bunch dried, natural
triticale*

· · ·

*1 bunch dried, natural
linseed*

· · ·

*1 bunch dried, natural
Nigella orientalis*

· · ·

*1 bunch dried, natural
phalaris*

· · ·

scissors

· · ·

.71 wires

· · ·

*1 straw plait, approximately
60 cm (24 in) long*

· · ·

twine

· · ·

raffia

*Although a good deal of
wiring is required for the
construction of this swag, it is
relatively straightforward and
enjoyable to make.*

T his harvest swag is a symbolic collection of dried decorative grasses. It relies on
the subtlety of colour differences and textural variation in the grasses for its
natural, yet splendid, effect.

In a church at harvest time the swag could be hung on a wall, or a series of
them could be mounted on the ends of the pews. In the home it could be hung
on a wall, or extended to decorate a mantelpiece.

1 Split each bunch of grass into 8 smaller
bunches, giving you 32 individual
bunches. Cut the stems to approximately
15 cm (6 in) long and double leg mount
the individual groups with .71 wires.

2 Start by tying a wired bunch of
triticale to the bottom of the plait
with the twine. Then place a bunch of
linseed above, to the left and slightly
overlapping the triticale, and bind this on
to the plait with the twine. Follow this
with a bunch of *Nigella orientalis* above, to
the right, and slightly overlapping the
triticale. Finish the sequence by
positioning a bunch of phalaris directly
above the triticale, slightly overlapping,
and bind on with the twine.

3 Repeat this pattern eight times to use
all four varieties of grasses, binding
each bunch on to the plait with the twine.

4 When all the grasses have been used
and the top of the plait reached, tie off
with the twine and trim any excess wires.

5 Make a bow from the raffia and tie it
on to the top of the decorated plait,
covering the wires and the twine.

HARVEST WREATH

· · ·

MATERIALS

· · ·

27 dried sunflower heads

· · ·

.71 wires

· · ·

*florist's tape
(stem-wrap tape)*

· · ·

scissors

· · ·

*30 pieces dried fungus
(various sizes)*

· · ·

3 dried corn cobs

· · ·

large vine circlet

· · ·

raffia

Harvest time conjures up images of fruit, vegetables and ears of corn. This wreath of dried flowers has corn cobs as its harvest time reference point, visually reinforced with fungus, a less obvious autumn crop, and sunflowers, which in this form serve as a reminder of summer days gone by.

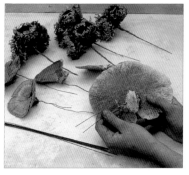

1 Single leg mount individual sunflower heads on .71 wires. Tape the stems, then group in threes. Double leg mount these groups with .71 wire and tape the stems. Double leg mount the pieces of fungus with .71 wire. You may need to cut the wire so that it has a sharp end to push through the fungus and twist into a double leg mount. Do not tape these wires.

2 Group the corn cobs at the bottom of the vine circlet and push their stems between the twisted vines, crossing them over each other to form a fan shape. Secure the corn cobs to each other and to the circlet with .71 wire.

3 Attach the groups of sunflowers, evenly spaced, all around the circumference of the circlet by pushing their wires through and wrapping tightly around the vines. These sunflower groups should alternate between the outside and inside edges of the vines.

4 Attach the fungus in groups of twos and threes around the circlet, between the sunflowers and around the corn cobs. The fungus groups should have the largest piece at the bottom with progressively smaller pieces above. Secure the fungus by straddling the vine with the legs of wire and twisting them together at the back.

5 Finally form a large bow from the raffia and tie it to the wreath over the stems of the corn cobs to conceal any remaining visible wires.

The large scale of this simple but unusual combination of materials gives the wreath great visual impact.

HALLOWEEN DISPLAY
. . .

MATERIALS
. . .
scissors
. . .
*15 slim branches autumn
leaves*
. . .
large ceramic pot
. . .
10 stems Chinese lanterns
. . .
10 stems red hot pokers
. . .
*10 stems orange lilies
'Avignon'*
. . .
20 stems antirrhinum

*This is a fine example of
creating a good shape in a large
display by using the natural
way the material would grow,
and without the support of
plastic foam or wire mesh. The
Halloween atmosphere is
completed by grouping
pumpkins and gourds,
intermingled with candles,
around the base of the
arrangement.*

Make this dramatic arrangement as a decoration for your Halloween party, and, for maximum impact, give it pride of place in a large room or entrance hall. The display is an intriguing mixture of materials in rich autumn colours; long-stemmed, two-coloured antirrhinums, Chinese lanterns, red hot pokers and orange lilies, all set against bright autumn foliage.

1 Cut the ends of the branches of autumn foliage at an angle of 45°, strip the bark from the bottom 5 cm (2 in) and split the branches about 5 cm (2 in) up the stems. Fill the pot with water and arrange the autumn foliage in it to create a fan-shaped outline. This fan must not be flat, and, to give it depth, bring shorter stems of foliage out from the back line into the front and centre of the shape.

2 Strip any leaves from the lower stems of the Chinese lanterns and arrange them throughout the foliage, reinforcing the overall shape. Distribute the red hot pokers throughout the display, again, using taller stems at the rear, and ones getting shorter towards the front.

3 The lilies are the focal flowers in this arrangement. Strip the lower leaves and distribute them throughout the display using taller, less open flowers towards the back and more open blooms on shorter stems around the centre and towards the front. Strip the lower antirrhinum leaves and arrange them evenly throughout the display.

CINNAMON ADVENT CANDLE

· · ·

MATERIALS

· · ·

*25 medium thickness
cinnamon sticks*

· · ·

*1 candle, 7.5 x 23 cm
(3 x 9¼ in)*

· · ·

raffia

· · ·

scissors

· · ·

*plastic foam ring for dried
flowers, 10 cm (4 in) diameter*

· · ·

.71 wires

· · ·

reindeer moss

· · ·

20 red rose heads

· · ·

florist's adhesive

*As a bonus, the heat of the
flame releases the spicy aroma
of the cinnamon, and the red
roses completes the festive look
of the candle.
Never leave a burning candle
unattended, and do not allow
the candle to burn down to
within 5 cm (2 in) of the
display height.*

Advent candles often have calibrations along their length to tell you how much to burn each day in the countdown to Christmas. This advent candle has a novel way of marking the passage of time: a spiral of 25 cinnamon sticks of decreasing height. Each day the candle is lit to burn down to the next cinnamon stick until finally on Christmas Day it is level with the shortest.

1 Attach the 25 cinnamon sticks to the outside of the candle by strapping them on with the raffia.

2 Position the cinnamon sticks in equal height reductions so that they spiral around the candle from the tallest at the top to the shortest at the bottom which should be approximately 6 cm (2¼ in) long. The excess lengths of cinnamon will be overhanging the bottom of the candle. Bind the cinnamon securely in place with raffia at two points and cut the excess lengths from the sticks so that they are all flush with the base of the candle.

3 Once the base is level, push the cinnamon-wrapped candle into the centre of the plastic foam ring. Make hairpin shapes from the .71 wires and pin the reindeer moss on to the foam to cover the ring completely.

4 Cut the stems of the dried roses to a length of approximately 2.5 cm (1 in). Add a little glue to the bases and stems of the roses. Push them into the plastic foam through the reindeer moss, to create a ring of rose heads around the candle.

CHRISTMAS ANEMONE URN
. . .

MATERIALS
. . .
1 small cast-iron urn
. . .
cellophane (plastic wrap)
. . .
1 block plastic foam
. . .
florist's adhesive tape
. . .
scissors
. . .
*1 bunch laurustinus
with berries*
. . .
10 stems bright orange roses
. . .
*20 stems anemones
('Mona Lisa' blue)*

The classic feel of a Christmas arrangement is retained by the use of the rusting cast-iron urn in which this spectacular display is set.

This vibrant display uses fabulously rich colours as an alternative to the traditional reds and greens of Christmas. An audacious combination of shocking orange roses set against the vivid purple anemones and the metallic blue berries of laurustinus makes an unforgettable impression.

1 Line the urn with the cellophane (plastic wrap). Soak the plastic foam in water and fit it into the lined urn, securing with the adhesive tape. Trim the cellophane around the rim of the urn.

2 Clean the stems of laurustinus and evenly arrange in the plastic foam to create a domed, all-round foliage framework within which the flowers will be positioned.

3 Distribute the roses, the focal flowers, evenly throughout the foliage, placing those with the most open blooms about two-thirds of the way up the arrangement, and more closed blooms towards the top.

4 Push the stems of anemones into the plastic foam amongst the roses, spreading them evenly throughout the arrangement so that a domed and regular shape is achieved.

TULIP AND HOLLY WREATH

· · ·

MATERIALS

· · ·

*plastic foam ring,
25 cm (10 in) diameter*

· · ·

100 stems white tulips

· · ·

scissors

· · ·

holly with berries

*The tulip stems are pushed
fully into the foam in tight
masses, so that only their heads
are visible.*

The extravagant use of white tulips achieves a sophisticated purity in this Christmas decoration. A cushion of white blooms interspersed with glossy dark green leaves and vibrant red berries produces a wreath that can be used either on a door or, with candles, as a table centrepiece.

1 Soak the plastic foam ring in water. Cut the tulips to a stem length of approximately 3 cm (1⅛ in). Starting at the centre, work outwards in concentric circles to cover the whole surface of the plastic foam with the tulip heads.

2 Cover any exposed foam and the outside of the ring with holly leaves by pushing their stems into the foam and overlapping them flat against the edge of the ring. (You may wish to secure the leaves with .71 wire.)

3 Cut 12 stems of berries approximately 4 cm (1½ in) long and push them into the foam in two concentric circles around the ring, one towards the inside and the other towards the outside. Make sure no foam is still visible.

CHRISTMAS CAKE DECORATION

• • •

If you're tired of decorating your Christmas cake in the same old way, with tinsel-edged paper, robins and snowmen stuck on top, be brave and go all out for a whole new look using natural materials! Combined with night-lights (tea-lights), this arrangement forms a memorable Christmas display.

MATERIALS

• • •

ribbon (width approximately
7.5 cm/3 in) in 2 patterns

• • •

3 10 cm (4 in) diameter
Christmas cakes

• • •

clear adhesive (sticky) tape

• • •

scissors

• • •

gold twine

• • •

1 glass cake stand

• • •

1 handful cranberries

• • •

1 handful small cones

• • •

4 purple tulip heads

• • •

7 red rose heads

• • •

1 stem small camellia leaves

• • •

gold dust powder

• • • •

3 night-lights (tea-lights)

1 Wrap the ribbon around the outside of each of the cakes and secure with a piece of clear adhesive tape. Tie the gold twine around the middle of each cake, over the ribbon, finishing with a bow at the front. This is both decorative and useful as it will hold the ribbon in place until the cakes are to be eaten.

2 Position the cakes on the stand and scatter cranberries and cones between them. Pull the petals from the tulips and the roses and scatter them among the cranberries and cones. Scatter camellia leaves similarly. Sprinkle a little gold dust powder over the petals and place the three night-lights (tea-lights) between the cakes.

Rather than one large cake this display uses a group of three small cakes which themselves become part of the decoration. The rich reds and purples of the flowers and fruit with green and gold trimmings combine lusciously with the night-lights (tea-lights). Never leave burning candles unattended.

CLEMENTINE WREATH

· · ·

MATERIALS

· · ·

.71 wires

· · ·

27 clementines

· · ·

*plastic foam ring, approximately
30 cm (12 in) diameter*

· · ·

pyracanthus berries and foliage

· · ·

ivy leaves

*The wreath will look
spectacular hung on a door or
wall, and can also be used as a
table decoration with a large
candle at its centre, or perhaps
a cluster of smaller candles of
staggered heights. The wreath
is very easy to make, but it is
heavy and if it is to be hung
on a wall or door, be sure to fix
it securely.*

This festive Christmas wreath is contemporary in its regular geometry and its bold use of materials and colours. Tightly-grouped seasonal clementines, berries and leaves are substituted for the traditional holly, mistletoe and pine. The wreath has a citrus smell, but can be made more aromatic by using bay leaves and other herbs instead of ivy.

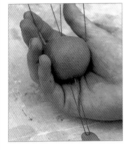

1 Push a .71 wire across and through the base of the clementine from one side to the other, and bend the two projected ends down. Bend another .71 wire to form a hairpin shape and push the ends right through the middle of the clementine so that the bend in the wire is sitting flush with the top of the fruit. Do the same to all the clementines. Cut all the projecting wires to a length of approximately 4 cm (1½ in).

2 Soak the plastic foam ring in water. Arrange the wired clementines in a tight circle on the top of the plastic ring by pushing their four projecting wire legs into the foam. Form a second ring of clementines within the first ring.

3 Cut the pyracanthus into small stems of berry clusters and foliage approximately 6 cm (2¼ in) long. Push the stems into the outer side of the plastic ring and between the two rings of clementines, making sure it is evenly distributed.

4 Cut the ivy leaves into individual stems measuring approximately 7 cm (2¾ in) in length. Push the stems of the individual leaves into the plastic ring, positioning a leaf between each clementine.

MISTLETOE KISSING RING
· · ·

MATERIALS
· · ·
scissors
· · ·
*7 berries-only stems of
winterberry*
· · ·
large bunch mistletoe
· · ·
twine
· · ·
1 twisted cane ring
· · ·
*1 roll tartan
(plaid) ribbon*

*Very simple in its construction
this design does require a
reasonable quantity of good
quality, fresh mistletoe for it to
survive the full festive season.*

Instead of just tying a bunch of mistletoe to some strategically placed light-fitting in the hall, be creative and make a traditional kissing ring. This can be hung up as a Christmas decoration and still serve as a focal point for a seasonal kiss!

1 Cut the stems of the winterberry into 18 cm (7 in) lengths. Divide the mistletoe into 14 substantial stems and make the smaller sprigs into bunches by tying with twine. Attach a branch of winterberry on to the outside of the ring with the twine. Add a stem, or bunch, of mistletoe so that it overlaps about one-third of the length of winterberry, and bind in place. Bind on another stem of winterberry, overlapping the mistletoe.

2 Repeat the sequence until the outside of the cane ring is covered in a "herringbone" pattern of materials. Cut four lengths of ribbon of approximately 60 cm (24 in) each. Tie one end of each of the pieces of ribbon to the decorated ring at four equidistant points around its circumference. Bring the four ends of the ribbon up above the ring and tie into a bow; this will enable you to suspend the finished kissing ring.

CHRISTMAS CANDLE TABLE DECORATION

· · ·

What could be more pleasing at Christmas, when the table is groaning under the weight of festive fare, than to complete the picture with a Christmas candle table decoration?

This rich display is a visual feast of the seasonal reds and greens of anemones, ranunculus and holly, softened by the grey of lichen on larch twigs and aromatic rosemary. The simple white candles are given a festive lift with their individual bows.

MATERIALS

· · ·

plastic foam ring,
25 cm (10 in) diameter

· · ·

25 cm (10 in) wire basket
with candleholders

· · ·

10 stems rosemary

· · ·

10 small stems lichen-covered
larch

· · ·

10 small stems holly

· · ·

scissors

· · ·

30 stems red anemones
('Mona Lisa')

· · ·

30 stems red ranunculus

· · ·

roll paper ribbon

· · ·

4 candles

The space at the centre of the
design is the perfect spot for
hiding those little, last-minute,
surprise presents!
Never leave burning candles
unattended and do not allow
the candles to burn below 5 cm
(2 in) of the display height.

1 Soak the plastic foam ring in water and wedge it snugly into the wire basket. You may need to trim the ring slightly, but make sure that you do not cut too much off by mistake.

2 Using a combination of rosemary, larch and holly, create an even but textured foliage and twig outline, all around the plastic foam ring. Make sure that the various foliages towards the outside edge of the display are shorter than those towards the centre.

3 Cut the stems of the anemones and ranunculus to 7.5 cm (3 in). Arrange them evenly throughout the display, leaving a little space around the candleholders. Make four ribbon bows and attach them to the candles. Position the candles in the holders.

CHRISTMAS TREE DECORATIONS

· · ·

MATERIALS

· · ·

*FOR STARS AND
CHRISTMAS TREES*
*1 block plastic foam
(for dried flowers)*

· · ·

knife

· · ·

shaped pastry cutters

· · ·

plastic bag

· · ·

loose, dried lavender

· · ·

gold dust powder

· · ·

florist's adhesive

· · ·

*loose, dried tulip and rose
petals*

· · ·

cranberries

· · ·

gold cord

· · ·

scissors

· · ·

*FOR DRIED FRUIT
DECORATIONS*
gold cord

· · ·

dried oranges and limes

· · ·

florist's adhesive

· · ·

dried red and yellow rose heads

· · ·

cinnamon sticks

As an alternative to commercially available Christmas tree decorations why not make your own? The decorations illustrated here use dried flower-arranging materials supplemented with some gold dust powder and seasonal cord and they are so easy to make you can even let the children help you.

1 For the stars and Christmas tree decorations, cut the block of plastic foam into approximately 3 cm (1 in) thick slices. Using the pastry cutters, press star and tree shapes from the plastic foam. Mix the dried loose lavender with two tablespoons of gold dust powder in a plastic bag (first making sure the bag has no holes in it), and shake together. Liberally coat all the surfaces of the plastic foam shapes with florist's adhesive.

2 Place the adhesive-covered shapes in the bag of lavender and gold dust powder, and shake. The shape will be coated with the lavender heads and powder. As a variation, press some of the dried tulip and rose petals on to the glue-covered shapes before putting them into the bag. Only the remaining exposed glued areas will then pick up the lavender. As a further variation, glue a cranberry to the centre of some of the stars. Make a small hole in the shape, pass gold cord through and make a loop with which to hang the decoration.

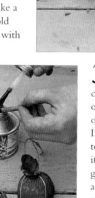

3 To make the dried fruit decorations, first tie the gold cord around the fruit, crossing it over at the bottom and knotting it on the top to make a hanging loop. Dab a blob of florist's adhesive on to the base of a rose head and stick it to the fruit next to the knotted gold cord at the top. Dab some adhesive on to two or three short pieces of cinnamon stick and glue these on to the dried fruit, grouping them with the rose head.

CHRISTMAS WIRE-MESH URN
• • •

MATERIALS
• • •
scissors
• • •
15 dried red rose heads
• • •
.38 silver wire
• • •
15 heads
Nigella orientalis
• • •
*15 small glycerined beech
leaves*
• • •
*75 small pieces cinnamon
stick, approximately 5 cm
(2 in) long*
• • •
gold-coloured cord
• • •
15 small bunches dried linseed
• • •
.71 wire
• • •
*florist's tape
(stem-wrap tape)*
• • •
1 wire-mesh urn
• • •
.32 silver reel (rose) wire
• • •
dried oranges and limes
• • •
gold dust powder

*The urn could be used for all
sorts of Christmas goodies to
brighten a table or sideboard
during the festive season.*

Sometimes we find odd things around the house which, with a little imagination, could be given a new lease of life. In this case an old wire-mesh urn has been turned into a seasonally decorated container for dried fruits.

1 Cut the rose stems and *Nigella orientalis* heads to 2.5 cm (1 in) and individually double leg mount them on .38 silver wires. Stitch wire the beech leaves with .38 silver wires. Tie the cinnamon into groups of five with the gold cord. Push a .38 silver wire around the cinnamon and under the cord. Make 15 bunches of linseed and double leg mount on .71 wires. Tape all the wired materials.

2 Take a bunch of linseed and lay it on the rim of the urn and bind on with .32 silver reel (rose) wire, passing the wire through the gaps in the mesh and pulling it tightly over the wired stem of the linseed and again through the mesh. Attach a rose head in the same way but slightly overlapping the linseed, and repeat this process with the grass head, the beech leaves and the cinnamon bundles.

3 Work continuously around the rim of the urn, always slightly overlapping the materials, until it is covered. Make sure that the materials come together neatly and there is no gap, then stitch the .32 silver reel (rose) wire through the mesh several times to secure finally. Fill the urn with the dried oranges and limes and scatter a little gold dust powder over the whole decoration.

ADVENT CANDLE WREATH

· · ·

An Advent wreath has four candles, one to be lit on each of the four Sundays leading up to Christmas Day.

This one is built on a pine foliage ring and uses fruits and spices for its decoration.

MATERIALS
· · ·
30 cm (12 in) blue pine foliage
ring
· · ·
45 x 30 cm (2 x 12 in)
candles
· · ·
scissors
· · ·
glue gun and glue sticks
· · ·
12 slices dried orange
· · ·
4 fresh clementines
· · ·
6 dried cut lemons
· · ·
5 dried whole oranges
· · ·
4 fir cones
· · ·
4 physallis heads
· · ·
16 short pieces cinnamon
stick
· · ·
ribbon
· · ·
.71 wires

1 Attach the four candles at equal distances around the circumference of the ring by cutting away some of the pine needles, putting hot glue on both the base of the candle and on the ring and pressing the two surfaces together for a few seconds. At the base of each candle glue an arrangement of the various materials. The orange slices and cinnamon sticks should be used in groups for the greatest effect.

This wreath is not complicated to make and can be used as a table decoration or, with ribbons, it could be hung in your hall.
Never leave burning candles unattended.

2 Make sure each candle has a selection of the materials at its base, spreading out around the ring.

3 Make four bows from the ribbon and bind with .71 wires at their centres. Attach these to the Advent wreath by pulling the two tails of .71 wire around the width of the ring, twisting them together underneath and returning the cut ends into the moss. Position one bow at each of the four central points between the candles. Make sure that the bows do not touch the candles..

GILDED FIG PYRAMID

· · ·

MATERIALS

· · ·

gilded terracotta plant pot

· · ·

*plastic foam cone for dried
flowers, approximately 25 cm
(10 in) high*

· · ·

40 black figs

· · ·

gilding paint

· · ·

.71 wires

· · ·

scissors

· · ·

50 ivy leaves

*This display has a powerful
impact that is disproportionate
to the simplicity of its
construction.*

This abundant use of figs produces a gloriously decadent decoration for a festive table. The deep purple figs with their dusting of gold, arranged with geometric precision, create an opulent yet architectural focal point for the most indulgent of occasions.

1 Make sure that the plastic foam cone sits comfortably in the pot. To ensure stability, you may wish to put a drop of adhesive around the edge of the cone base. Gild the figs slightly on one side of the fruit only, by rubbing the gilding paint on to the skin with your fingers.

2 Wire the gilded figs by pushing a .71 wire horizontally through the flesh approximately 2.5 cm (1 in) above the base of the fruit. Carefully bend the two protruding pieces of wire so that they point downwards. Do take care when wiring the figs or you could tear their skins.

3 Attach the figs to the cone by pushing their wires into the plastic foam. Work in concentric circles around the cone upwards from the bottom.

4 When the cone is covered, position the last fig on the tip of the plastic foam cone, with its stem pointing upwards to create a point.

5 Make hairpin shapes out of the .71 wires and pin the ivy leaves in to the cone between the gilded figs, covering any exposed foam.

INDEX

· · ·

NOTES

NOTES

Notes

NOTES

NOTES

NOTES

NOTES

NOTES